"**I**t's a *wonderful* book! Elvia Alvarado makes the connections so many have made, and are making, in the continental fight for survival. Medea Benjamin has done us a great service by giving us the voice of this Honduran woman."

—MARGARET RANDALL
Author, photographer, teacher

"**H**ere is a voice seldom heard, the voice of Latin America's majority, those who bear the burdens of society. If we are to understand Honduras, Central America, or, for that matter, Latin America, we must listen attentively to this voice. It has much to teach us. It commands the future."

—E. BRADFORD BURNS
Professor of History, UCLA

"**E**lvia's story provides the reader with a perspective on Honduras—indeed, on all of Central America—that even the best reporting from the outside cannot offer."

—MOST REVEREND JOHN R. QUINN
Archbishop of San Francisco

"**E**lvia Alvarado's insights are simple and penetrating. Her account of the life of a campesina is deeply moving, as is her courage and achievement."

—NOAM CHOMSKY
Professor and author

"**E**lvia Alvarado speaks as a woman, a mother, and as a peasant organizer. Her story tells of the courageous efforts of peasant communities to obtain such basic needs as land, food, education, and health care. It is an important contribution to the firsthand accounts that communicate the everyday effects of political and social forces."

—ISABEL LETELIER
Chilean human rights activist

"**T**his peasant woman's touching and open account can help us understand why the turmoil in Central America is not an East-West conflict, but a metaphor for first and third world disparities."

DR. CHARLIE CLEMENTS
Author, *Witness to War*

DON'T BE AFRAID, GRINGO

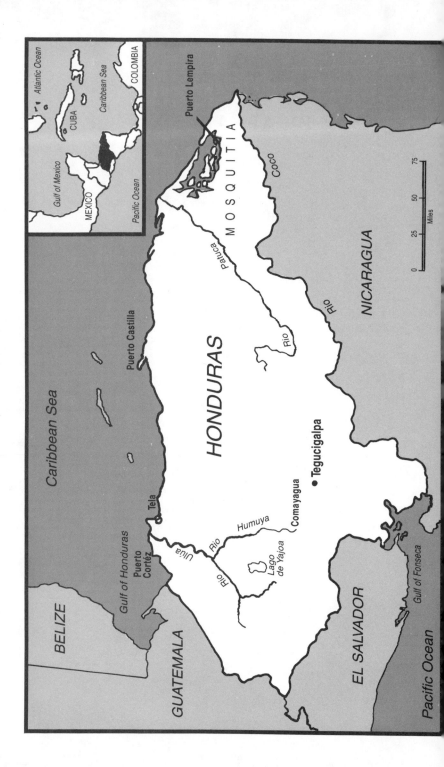

DON'T BE AFRAID, GRINGO

A Honduran Woman Speaks from the Heart

THE STORY OF ELVIA ALVARADO
Translated and Edited by Medea Benjamin

Food First

A FOOD FIRST BOOK
The Institute for Food and Development Policy
145 Ninth Street, San Francisco, CA 94103

Printed in the United States of America

10 9 8 7 6 5 4 3 2

To order additional çopies of this book, please write:
The Institute for Food and Development Policy
145 Ninth Street
San Francisco, CA 94103
(415) 864-8555

Please add 15 percent for postage and handling ($1 minimum).
California residents add sales tax. Bulk discounts available.

Photos: Copyright © Susan Meiselas/Magnum Photos, Inc.
Design: Cecilia Brunazzi
Typesetting: Graphion

Table of Contents

Dedicated to the memory of Benjamin Linder and to the many thousands who keep his vision alive by extending a hand of friendship to the poor of Central America.

Acknowledgments

First and foremost, I want to thank Elvia's wonderful family and the National Congress of Rural Workers (CNTC) for taking the risk this book implies. I only hope that the book helps to further their vital quest for justice in Honduras.

I'd also like to thank the staff of the Institute for Food and Development Policy—Food First—for their continuing support of this project. I'm especially grateful to Becky Buell, Ann Clark, Jon Christensen, Andrea Freedman, Ann Kelly, Kathie Klarreich, Diana Markel, Frances Moore Lappé, Kirsten Mueller, and my mother, Rose Benjamin, for their invaluable comments and suggestions. Special thanks to editor Meredith Maran and copy editor Frieda Werden, and Food First interns Tony Mack, Debbie Stone, and Mindy Williams.

For the beautiful photos, I'm indebted to photographer Susan Meiselas, who gave of her precious time and talent to help make Elvia come alive to the readers.

I'd also like to acknowledge the insightful conversations in Honduras with Juan Almendares, Ramón Custodio, Gautama Fonseca, and our colleagues at the Honduran Documentation Center (CEDOH). In the United States, I'm indebted to Eric Weaver of the Central America Resource Center, Eric Shultz and Roxanna Pastor of the Honduras Information Center, and Philip Shepherd for his brilliant work on Honduras.

I'm especially grateful to Pueblo to People, whose founders Dan Salcedo and Marijke Velzeboer first introduced me to Elvia, and whose work with Honduran cooperatives provides an inspiration to those of us trying to develop a new kind of partnership with our Central American neighbors.

This book would not be possible without the 20,000 members of the Institute for Food and Development Policy. Their contributions, large and small, allow us to seek out people like Elvia Alvarado and give them a voice here in the United States. I also gratefully acknowledge the Max and Anna Levinson Foundation for their support of this project.

Special thanks to my husband Kevin Danaher and daughter Arlen Siu for enduring the many trips away from home and making that home such a wonderful place to come back to.

And most of all, thanks to Elvia Alvarado for allowing us to pry into the nooks and crannies of her life, so that we may share her pain, her suffering, her hopes, and her dreams.

MEDEA BENJAMIN

Foreword

When you first came to my house, I was afraid to talk to you. "What is this *gringa* doing here in my house, the house of a poor campesina?" I wondered. Because when you said you were from the United States, I thought you were from the U.S. military base, from Palmerola. And since I thought all gringos were the same, I thought you had come here to do me harm.

You said you came to learn my story, to learn from me what the campesino struggle was all about.

I thought about our struggle, how we suffer hunger, persecution, abuse by the landowners. How we fight with all the bureaucrats at the National Agrarian Institute. How we fight with the police, the army, the security forces.

I'd just been released from jail four days ago. I'd been arrested many times before, when we've tried to get a piece of land for the poor campesinos to farm. But for the first time in my life I was tortured. Simply because I work for justice and speak the truth.

So here comes this gringa asking me to tell our story. "Why should I get myself in more trouble?" I said to myself. "Better keep quiet and send this gringa back where she came from."

But then I decided that I couldn't pass up a chance to tell the world our story. Because our struggle is not a secret one, it's an open one. The more people who know our story the better. Even if you are a gringa, I thought, once you understand why we're fighting, if you have any sense of humanity, you'll have to be on our side.

ELVIA ALVARADO

Introduction

It is now accepted as a truism by even the most conservative pundits that poverty is the seedbed of rebellion. In the case of Central America, the revolutionary upheavals racking the region are rooted in the dire poverty of the majority. In Guatemala, El Salvador, and pre-revolutionary Nicaragua, thousands of impoverished *campesinos* (peasants) took up arms because they had nothing to lose. As a campesino in El Salvador told us, "Better to die from a bullet than to die the slow death of hunger."

But Honduras, the poorest country in Central America and the second poorest in the hemisphere, proves the point that poverty alone is not enough to spawn rebellion. Apart from minor, sporadic bursts of guerrilla activity over the years, Honduras has remained relatively free of armed conflict.

How is it that Honduras has managed to escape the violent confrontations that have engulfed neighboring El Salvador, Nicaragua, and Guatemala?

If people are poor but so are all their neighbors, then poverty is more likely to be attributed to the design of God than the hand of man. In Guatemala, Nicaragua, and El Salvador, the extremes of wealth and poverty existed side by side. But Honduras had no dictator comparable to Somoza, who owned over 20 percent of Nicaragua's land as well as many factories and businesses. It had no equivalent of El

Salvador's "14 families" or Guatemala's infamously rich oligarchy.

In Honduras the majority of the nation's wealth rested in the hands of foreign companies—United Fruit, Standard Fruit, Rosario Mining Company—and ended up in U.S. bank accounts. Hondurans joke that their country is so poor it can't even afford an oligarchy.

This is not to say that wealth—or more correctly, poverty—is evenly distributed. A 1979 survey of household income found that the poorest 20 percent of the population received 3.5 percent of the income, while the wealthiest 20 percent garnered 56 percent.[1] The rural areas are much more depressed than the cities. A 1984 study revealed that 88 percent of the rural population had a monthly income of less than $25 per person.[2] But historically, the inequalities in Honduras have been less glaring than those in neighboring countries.[3]

Another reason why poor Hondurans have not resorted to armed struggle is that over the years they have managed to wrest important concessions from the government through peaceful means. A 1954 strike against the United Fruit Company pulled 35,000 workers off the plantations and docks, and forced the government to recognize unions, collective bargaining, and the right to strike.

In the aftermath of the strike, organizing among workers and campesinos blossomed, and the Honduran work force soon became the best organized in Central America. The workers' collective strength made them important actors in national politics and forced a series of governments to pay heed to their demands for land and better working conditions.

The two most important reform governments were that of Ramón Villeda Morales (1958–1963) and the military regime of Walter López Arellano (1972–1975). Their governments instituted a labor code, social security, and—most essential for the campesino majority—land reform.

The first land reform, decreed in 1962, was quite mild. Vociferous opposition from the banana companies forced the government to weaken it to the point where only state land could be redistributed. But reforms in 1972 and 1975 were more radical. They stipulated that all land—whether state or private—had to fulfill a "social function." If land was lying idle or was in some way poorly used, it was to be expropriated and turned over to landless campesinos.

But as Elvia Alvarado's story dramatically illustrates, these reforms looked better on the books than they did in practice. For example, the 1975 land reform aimed at distributing 600,000 hectares of land to 120,000 campesino families within five years. But a 1980 study found that at the rate the land was actually distributed, it would take 103 years to reach its five-year goal.[4]

Nevertheless, just the fact that these reforms were the official law of the land drastically altered the relationship between the government and the poor. Rather than fighting to overthrow the government, as was happening in neighboring countries, the poor of Honduras were fighting to force their government to uphold its own laws. They had a stake in the system; their struggle was to make that system work in their favor.

Perhaps the most critical factor in determining whether people will take up arms is how the military responds to their nonviolent struggles. When campesinos and workers are gunned down in the street during peaceful demonstrations, when attempts to organize the poor are treated as subversive acts, when leaders of unions and popular organizations are whisked out of their homes in the middle of the night never to be heard from again, taking up arms becomes a question of self-defense. This has been the case at various periods in the history of Nicaragua, El Salvador, and Guatemala.

In Honduras the military has been generally more restrained—with some significant exceptions. The most savage attack was the Olancho massacre of 1975, when 14 campesinos and activists were brutally tortured and murdered. Nine of their dismembered bodies were later found burned and stuffed in a well.

Rather than being considered "par for the course," such atrocities were national scandals in Honduras. The military was not supposed to be the enemy of the people. Long after the poor of Guatemala, Nicaragua, and El Salvador began to regard men in uniform with fear and loathing, the poor of Honduras still had a modicum of faith in their armed forces.

In sum, Honduras was spared the armed revolts that have devastated its neighbors because it was less socially stratified, because the poor had a stake in the system, and because its military was more civilized in dealing with internal dissent.

But events in the 1980s that thrust Honduras deeply into the Central American imbroglio began to erode the nation's stabilizing characteristics, making Honduras more and more analogous to its troubled neighbors.

Honduras in the 1980s

U.S. Senator James Sasser (D–Tennessee), the chairman of the Appropriations Subcommittee on Military Construction, described his visit to Honduras in early 1984:

> An Army Blackhawk helicopter carried us through a mountain pass and over a lush jungle valley. In a few moments, the jungle cleared to reveal an 8,000-foot runway, newly constructed by the U.S. Army Combat Engineers, and a complex of tents and wooden jungle barracks. I was struck by the similarity of this scene to those of 20 years ago in Southeast Asia. But this was not Thailand or Vietnam. It was Honduras.

In the 1980s Honduras, once the sleepy backwater of Central America, suddenly became the nerve center for U.S. policy in the region. The Sandinistas were in power in Nicaragua, and in El Salvador the growing strength of the Farabundo Martí National Liberation Front (FMLN) threatened to topple the U.S.-backed Salvadoran government. The U.S. government, appalled by the specter of left-wing governments in its "back yard," saw Honduras as key to its geopolitical interests.

In exchange for vast increases in U.S. military and economic aid, Honduras joined hands with the United States in its effort to topple the Sandinistas in Nicaragua. Honduras became a base for the Nicaraguan rebel force, the "contras," and its army provided logistical and intelligence support to the Salvadoran military in its war against the FMLN guerrillas.[6]

To fulfill its regional military role, the United States turned Honduras into an armed camp. Since 1980, the U.S. military has built or improved eleven airstrips, two sophisticated radar stations, several base camps and training facilities, combat-ready helicopter refueling pads, and a large-scale command and logistics center at Palmerola Air Base.

U.S. military aid to Honduras jumped sixteenfold between 1980 and 1986.[7] So massive was the U.S.-sponsored military buildup that even CIA operatives and U.S. embassy officials began to cynically refer to Honduras as the "Pentagon Republic" or "USS Honduras."

The first casualty of this militarization was the incipient process of democratization. U.S. policy initially aimed at making Honduras a showplace democracy in Central America. After nearly 18 years of military rule, the United States pressured the Honduran military to hold elections in 1981. The elections were relatively open and honest, but they failed to bring Honduras any closer to democracy because the military maintained a firm grip on the reins of power.

Before the elections, both major candidates met with the military chiefs and agreed to give the armed forces veto power over all cabinet appointments and full control over security issues, including the right to determine policy toward Nicaragua and El Salvador.[8] As Dr. Ramón Custodio, head of the Honduran Human Rights Commission, asserted, "They [the military] have retired from the front office for reasons of protocol. But as far as power is concerned, they are and will continue to remain in the front office."[9]

The strengthening of Honduras's military produced a parallel weakening of civilian power. As Lt. Col. John Buchanan of the Center for Development Policy stated in testimony before the U.S. Congress, "U.S. military aid to Honduras strengthens the hands of those who are most likely to terminate democratic government in that country."[10] The electoral process, rather than curbing the power of the military, allowed the military to act with greater impunity now that it was covered by the facade of a civilian government.

The most tragic sign of the militarization of Honduran society was an alarming rise in human rights abuses. While before 1980 there was never a systematic policy of repression, from 1981 to 1984 there were 218 political assassinations, 110 disappearances, and 1,947 illegal detentions.[11]

For the first time in its history, Honduras became the scene of disappearances, outright political assassinations, secret cemeteries, and clandestine detention centers. Torture of prisoners became routine. In 1983 Honduras joined the exclusive United Nations list of countries that "arbitrarily execute people."[12]

Opposition to U.S. influence or to the presence of the contras on Honduran soil was treated as heresy. Journalist Rodrigo Wong Arevalo, a critic of Honduran foreign policy, narrowly missed being killed when a bomb exploded in his car. Gasoline bombs were thrown into the office of the Honduran Human Rights Committee. A death list circulated with the names of 17 prominent opposition politicians, intellectuals, and labor leaders.

The head of the armed forces in 1986, General Regalado Hernández, charged that anyone who defamed the contras, protested U.S. presence in Honduras, or brought up the question of disappeared persons was part of a communist conspiracy.

This clampdown had a devastating effect on the "popular organizations," as they are called in Latin America: trade unions, campesino groups, student and professional associations. The most outspoken leaders, such as Rolando Vindel of the electrical company union and Cristóbal Pérez of the Federation of Honduran Workers, were gunned down or disappeared. An "anti-terrorist" law was passed in 1982, under which traditional forms of protest such as land takeovers, factory occupations, and street demonstrations were labeled subversive and carried stiff jail sentences.

The government employed a wide array of tactics to disarm the popular organizations. Elections were rigged, leaders were corrupted through massive infusions of money (most of it from U.S. government aid programs), and the government fomented divisions by pitting one group against the other.

For example, the National Campesino Union (UNC), once the most militant and outspoken of the campesino groups, fell into the hands of more conservative leaders who collaborated with the government in an attempt to break the militant agrarian reform workers' union (SITRAINA). Government interference also ensured that the United Fruit workers' union, the university students' union, and the teachers' union all came under the control of conservative, pro-government factions.

The heavy influx of U.S. dollars that accompanied the militarization process created a gold-rush atmosphere, which aggravated the endemic corruption and infighting within the Honduran military. A 1986 U.S. government study reported that between November 1985 and January 1986 over one million dollars of Congressional funds designated to aid the contras were diverted to the Honduran military.[13] An October 1986 shake-up in the military in which 30 high-ranking officers were fired was linked to the U.S. Congressional passage of $100 million in contra aid. A Western diplomat commented, "With all of this money around, where you are in the command structure becomes far more strategic if you want to line your pockets."[14]

As the military chiefs and politicians were getting rich off U.S. aid, the majority of Hondurans were getting poorer, for the 1980s also marked the beginning of a severe economic crisis. The falling world market prices for Honduran commodities—bananas, coffee, cotton, sugar—reduced export earnings. Payment on the growing foreign debt ate up larger and larger chunks of the government budget. The regional crisis led to a virtual paralysis of private investment, and by 1986 unemployment had shot up to a whopping 41 percent.[15]

The only flourishing sector of the economy was the military. At a time when government social services were more crucial than ever to cushion the impact of the economic crunch, the burgeoning military budget was eating away at social expenditures. Between 1986 and 1987, the already inadequate health budget was further reduced from $130 million to $97 million. Former Finance Minister Manuel Acosta deplored the detrimental effect the military buildup was having on social spending. "The cutbacks," he lamented, "are bringing the population to a point of desperation. My worry is that we are in fact provoking a situation of violence and an internal rebellion by our very neglect of these basic needs of the people."[16]

The irony of U.S. policy in Honduras is that in the name of preserving democracy, the United States has managed to polarize Honduran society as never before. The conditions that once set Honduras apart from its neighbors are quickly vanishing. There is more ostentatious wealth, with generals and politicians living high on the hog; there is more corruption, with vicious power struggles over the spoils of U.S. aid money; there is greater poverty as the military consumes more and more of the government budget; and there is more repression and less room for peaceful dissent.

Why Elvia Alvarado?

It is one thing to look at the regional crisis and the role of Honduras in geopolitical terms. But what does it mean to the Honduran people, the majority of whom are poor campesinos? How has it affected their everyday lives?

I had been to Honduras many times; but like so many others, I had sought out the opinions of politicians, academics, and professionals. So in the summer of 1986 I returned to learn from ordinary Hondurans. I interviewed dozens of people from all walks of life—campesinos, factory workers, rural mothers, health workers, priests.

One of the interviews stood out from the rest: the interview with Elvia Alvarado, a 48-year-old mother of six, grandmother of eleven. Elvia works as a campesina organizer with the National Congress of Rural Workers, the CNTC. She travels throughout the back roads of the country, helping dirt-poor campesinos in their struggles to feed themselves. She is an eloquent spokeswoman on the plight of the poor and their self-help efforts to overcome their poverty.

Elvia also has firsthand experience with the recent militarization of her country. For one thing, she lives near the largest U.S. base in Central America, the Palmerola Air Base, which has a constant presence of at least 1,000 U.S. troops. But Elvia's connection with the military goes deeper than that. As a result of her organizing work, she has been harassed, jailed, and most recently, tortured, at the hands of the Honduran military. She has witnessed the parallel growth of internal repression and the U.S. military buildup.

Elvia's story is by no means that of a typical campesina. Through her organizing work, she has had the opportunity to travel around her country, talking not only to campesinos but also to lawyers, professors, politicians. She has gained insights into the internal workings of her society that far surpass those of a campesino who has never ventured from his or her village. But Elvia does represent the hopes and dreams of the campesinos, and has devoted her life to making those dreams a reality.

The story was pieced together from some 30 hours of taped interviews. Elvia insisted that we conduct the interviews while visiting some of the campesino groups she works with. "If you really want to understand what I'm saying," she said, "you'll have to go out with me and see where I work, how I get there, where I sleep, how the people I work with live. Otherwise you'll never know if I'm telling the truth."

So off we went. We hiked into the mountains to visit far-flung rural communities, and returned again with the well-known international photographer Susan Meiselas. We slept out in the cornfields and on the floors of campesino shacks. We visited women's groups, rural clinics, community schools, parish priests. We jumped government barricades to join a striking union. We marched in the capital with the campesinos in a massive demonstration against the contra presence.

The more time we spent together, the more Elvia opened up. Once her initial mistrust of gringos faded, her stories gained greater detail, her language grew more descriptive. I had no trouble getting her to talk. On the contrary. After a long, weary day of traveling and meetings, she would nudge me to turn on the tape recorder. "Hurry up," she'd say. "I just remembered something important and I don't want to lose it." I was no longer the interviewer writing a book on Elvia. It was Elvia's book. It was her way of communicating with the outside world.

Just when the book was about to go to press, we got word that her organization, the CNTC, was having second thoughts about the project. There was an increased climate of fear in Honduras. Death threats were circulating with the names of government critics, and groups like Elvia's CNTC were under attack.

The CNTC was anxious for the book to come out; they placed great importance on getting their message to a wide audience. But at the same time they worried that the book might put Elvia's life in jeopardy. They wondered if it might be better to publish the story anonymously, without Elvia's name or photos.

Together with Elvia and the CNTC, we at Food First immediately began to rethink the entire project. We sought the advice of numerous human rights groups in Honduras and the United States, and debated the pros and cons. If we published the book without Elvia's name but with the story intact, it would still be easy for the Honduran authorities to discern the protagonist. And if we changed the text enough to mask Elvia's imprint, it would no longer be the compelling story it is.

On the other hand, we all knew that Elvia was already on the military's blacklist because of the nature of her organizing work. The human rights groups we consulted agreed that the only measure that might provide Elvia a modicum of protection was international recognition, especially from the United States.

We decided that the best way to both publicize the issues and protect Elvia's life was to go public, but create a network of concerned groups and individuals to watch out for her safety. We also decided to disguise the names of many of the other characters mentioned in the book—those who might be hurt by their mere association with Elvia.

Elvia has increased the peril to her own life by telling us her story. But she has not taken this risk for nothing; she is asking us for something in return. She is asking us to take a stand, as she has. She is asking us to speak out, as she has. She is asking us to take risks, as she has. In essence, this book is Elvia's plea for us to join her in the struggle to create a new Central America, one in which a poor campesina's life will not be endangered merely because she dares to work for justice and to speak the truth.

May 1987   MEDEA BENJAMIN

NOTES

1. Study by CONSUPLANE, the Honduran economic planning agency, cited by Robert Macdonald in "From those who have not, even what they think they have will be taken away," *Honduras Update,* October 1985, p. 5.
2. Mario Ponce Cambar, "Honduras: Política agrícola y perspectivas," in *Honduras: Realidad nacional y crisis regional* (Tegucigalpa: Centro de Documentación de Honduras, 1986), p. 257.
3. A comparative study of land distribution using 1960s data found that Honduras was the least skewed of all Central America. See Charles Lewis Taylor and Michael C. Hudson, *World Manual of Social and Political Indicators* (New Haven: Yale University Press, 1972).
4. Instituto Hondureño de Desarrollo Rural, *84 meses de reforma agraria del Gobierno de las Fuerzas Armadas de Honduras* (Tegucigalpa: IHDR, 1980), pp. 258–9.

5. James R. Sasser, "The Country Is Becoming an Armed Camp," *Wall Street Journal*, March 9, 1984.

6. Despite the traditional enmity between El Salvador and Honduras since the 1969 "Soccer War," the Honduran military has provided key support to their Salvadoran counterparts. They allowed Salvadoran soldiers to enter Honduran territory in pursuit of guerrillas, and went so far as to participate in the macabre massacres of hundreds of Salvadoran refugees who were crossing the Sumpul and Lempa rivers in search of refuge. On U.S. insistence, Salvadoran soldiers were trained on Honduran soil (until popular pressure forced the closing of the training center in 1985), and the San Lorenzo Air Base in southern Honduras was loaned to the Salvadoran military for intelligence-gathering flights over guerrilla territory.

7. Military aid went from $3.9 million in 1980 to $77.4 million in 1984, dropping to $61.2 million in 1986 due to budget cuts. See *AID Congressional Presentation FY 1988*, main vol. (Washington, DC: Agency for International Development, 1987), p. 872.

8. Philip L. Shepherd, "Honduras," in *Confronting Revolution: Security Through Diplomacy in Central America*, ed. Morris Blachman, et al. (New York: Pantheon, 1986), p. 130.

9. Philip E. Wheaton, *Inside Honduras: Regional Counterinsurgency Base* (Washington, DC: EPICA [Ecumenical Program for Inter-American Communication and Action], 1982), p. 53.

10. John Buchanan, "Statement before the Subcommittee on Inter-American Affairs of the U.S. House of Representatives, Washington, DC, September 21, 1982" (Washington, DC: Center for Development Policy, n.d.), p. 14.

11. Honduran Committee for the Defense of Human Rights (CODEH), cited in *Honduras Update*, October 1984, p. 2.

12. Personal interview with Ramón Custodio, director of CODEH, August 20, 1986.

13. General Accounting Office Report, *Humanitarian Assistance to the Nicaraguan Democratic Resistance* (Washington, DC: GPO, June 11, 1986).

14. Tim Golden, "Pro-Contra Officers Lose Out in Honduran Infighting," *Miami Herald*, October 3, 1986.

15. CODEH, "Conflictos laborales," *Boletín Informativo*, No. 62. June 1986, p. 2. This is the figure given by the prestigious Honduran Economists' Association. The government unemployment figure for 1986 was 25 percent.

16. Manuel Acosta, statement on *Morning Edition*, National Public Radio, April 11, 1984.

"*I never really had much of a childhood at all. By the time I was 13, I was already on my own.*"

Elvia with two of her daughters and grandchildren.

1

Childhood to Motherhood

My father was a campesino. He didn't have any land of his own, so he worked for the big landowners as a day worker. My mother raised chickens and pigs, and baked bread to sell at the market. They had seven children—five girls and two boys.

By the time I was six years old, I knew that my parents didn't get along. One of the problems was that there wasn't much work for my father. He'd go looking for work every day, but most of the time he didn't find anything. So he'd go out and get drunk instead. Then he'd come home and pick fights with my mother and hit her with his machete.

My mother would keep quiet when my father hit her. She knew that if she opened her mouth, if she dared to argue with him, he'd hit her more. But we kids would cry and scream and beg him to stop.

My mother finally decided that she couldn't take such abuse any longer, and she left him when I was seven.

After we left, my father moved to the coast. We never saw him again. Years later, after I had my first child, we got a telegram saying he had died. He was buried out there on the coast.

My mother worked like a mule to take care of us, and we all helped out. We'd get up at three in the morning, in the dark, to help bake bread, make tortillas, feed the pigs, and clean the house. All my brothers and sisters worked hard—the boys in the fields of the big landowners, the girls in our house. At the age of seven, we were all working.

My father never let my older sisters go to school. He couldn't see why girls needed an education, since they'd only go live with a man and have babies. But my mother wanted us to learn, and since I was still young enough she decided to send me to school.

I was in school from the time I was seven until I was 12, but I only finished second grade. That's because the school in the town where I grew up only went to second grade. But I really wanted to learn, so I kept repeating second grade over and over again—five times—since there was nowhere else for me to go.

I can't say I had a happy childhood. We didn't have any toys; we didn't have time for games. We were too busy for that, since we were always working.

The only happy moments I recall were the dances on Saturdays, when my mother let me go dancing with my girlfriends. There'd be guitar players in the village square, and on special occasions they'd bring in a marimba band.

The other thing I liked was going to church. On Sundays we'd go to catechism class; we'd sing religious songs and learn the prayers. Sometimes the priest would make *piñatas* for us in the square. All the kids in the catechism class would get candy, bananas, and sodas. That was a big treat for us.

I never really had much of a childhood at all. By the time I was 13, I was already on my own. My mother went to live with a man in town. He didn't want to take care of her children, so she left us behind in the village. I wouldn't say she abandoned us; it's just one of those things that happens in life. She kept coming around to see how we were. To this day my mother always comes by my house to see how we're doing.

But it was hard when she first left us. I went to live with my older brother, who was married and had his own family.

My brother no longer talks to me because of the work I do. He works for one of the big landowners, and he calls me a communist because I try to organize the campesinos that don't have any land. But when I first went to live with his family, he treated me well.

After I'd been living with my brother for about two years, I started going out with a boy named Samuel. We were both 15 years old and didn't know what we were doing. When we fooled around, I had no idea I'd get pregnant—but I did. In those days, no one ever taught us the facts of life. The adults said that children weren't supposed to learn about such things. So we were left to figure it out on our own.

I remember that the first time I got my period I was terrified. I saw that my vagina was bleeding from the inside. I ran into the woods to take off my panties and look at the blood. I went back home, got a pail from the kitchen, and went to bathe myself. I thought that maybe taking a bath would stop the bleeding. But I just kept bleeding and bleeding.

I was so scared that I stuck some rags in my panties and laid down in the bed. I wrapped the blanket around me, covering myself from head to foot.

My mother came in and asked what was wrong, but I was too ashamed to tell her. I said I had a headache, but she knew I was lying. After I'd been in bed for a few hours, she finally said, "OK. You better tell me what's wrong, or else get out of bed and get back to work."

So I told her I was bleeding between my legs. "Don't be scared," she said. "All women get the same thing. It'll last about three days and then go away." When I got the same thing the next month, I wasn't so scared because at least I knew what it was.

Nowadays, the kids learn these things in school. But when I was young nobody told us anything.

Anyway, when my brother found out I was pregnant, he was furious. He said he was going to kill me. I hid in my older sister's house and he went there looking for me. When she told him I wasn't there, he said, "OK. Tell that little slut that I'll be back, and that I'm going to get her with the six bullets I have left in my gun. Because I don't like what she's done to me. I've taken care of her for two years, and look how she's repaid me."

My sister came back crying. She'd never seen my brother so mad. "You better get out of here quick," she said. "The best thing you can do is go to the capital where he won't be able to find you."

I didn't know what to do. I was only 15, and I'd never been to the capital before. I'd never even been to Comayagua, which is just a short bus ride away. What on earth would I do in the capital all by myself?

I wrapped my two dresses in a piece of cloth—that was my suitcase. I was barefoot because I didn't even own a pair of shoes at that time. My sister gave me the money for the bus fare, and I took off for the capital.

When I got off the bus, I didn't know where to go and I didn't have any money. I asked someone where the nearest park was, and I went and sat down on the park bench. I was three months pregnant, and my stomach was just beginning to show.

I sat on the bench for hours, crying and crying. I kept thinking, "What in the world will become of me? Where can I go? How am I going to eat? Where am I going to sleep?" It was getting dark. People kept walking by and staring at me.

At about 11 p.m., the caretaker of the park came and asked me why I was sitting there so long. I told him I was just relaxing, but he said, "You've been here for hours. I saw you when I came on at 6 o'clock and it's now 11. What's wrong?" He looked at my bundle. "You're not from here, are you?"

I told him I was from Lejamani, and that I was sitting in the park because I'd never been to the city before and I didn't know where else to go. I said I was exhausted and asked if I could spend the night in the park.

He said, yes, I could sleep in the park, and that he would watch me and make sure nothing happened to me. I put my bundle under my head as a pillow and fell asleep.

Early in the morning I woke up to the sounds of the women setting up their stalls in the market nearby. They were lighting fires to warm up coffee and milk for breakfast. I sat on the bench watching them. I was starving but I didn't have a cent.

The caretaker saw me and came over. "You don't have any money, do you?" he said. "Here, take this and buy yourself some bread and a cup of coffee." He gave me 50 cents (one *lempira*).

When the caretaker's shift was over, he warned me, "Look, muchacha, another man will be coming on now. He's not like me, and he might not let you stay here."

So I left. I put my bundle under my arm and started ringing doorbells, asking for work. But I was dirty and dressed in rags, so no one wanted to give me work. I walked up and down the streets, day and night, but couldn't find anything.

In the evening I went back to the park after the same caretaker returned for the night shift. I slept in the park again and began knocking on doors the next day. At the end of the second day, I found work.

I was hired as a cook in someone's house. It was a husband and wife with two children. The woman hired me because she realized I was pregnant and felt sorry for me. She said she'd pay me $10 a month, and I could stay there until I had my baby. But after that I'd have to leave, because she didn't want a baby in the house.

I worked there for six months. The woman was good to me, and every month I'd save the $10 I earned so I'd have money to buy things for my baby.

Some women have all kinds of problems when they get pregnant—they get nauseous and lose their appetite, or they have headaches and get real tired. Not me. The only way I ever know I'm pregnant is because I don't get my period. Otherwise I have no other signs.

I worked right up to the last day. When I started getting bad pains, I told the woman I worked for and she took me to the hospital.

I didn't know anything, because it was my first child. But when I felt the labor pains, I just gritted my teeth and clenched my fists until it passed. I didn't cry or anything.

The nurse said, "When you get a really strong pain that doesn't go away fast, push so the baby comes out."

She showed me this cement board they strap you on with your legs wide open—with everything sticking out. She said I should use it when the baby was ready to come out.

I had these pains, and they'd come and go, come and go. Then they started coming faster and faster, until I got this big pain that wouldn't go away. I said to myself, "Ah-ha. This must be what the nurse was talking about."

So I ran over to the board, stuck my legs in the stirrups, and pushed hard. I felt something wet coming out first. And then I felt the baby zooming out, like water rushing out of a bottle when you take the top off. The baby started crying, and one of the other pregnant women ran to tell the nurse.

The nurse came running over, furious. "Why didn't you call me?" she yelled. "You're not supposed to do this on your own." She grabbed the baby, cut his cord, and stuck him in a tub of water.

I don't know why she was so mad. She never told me to call for help, so how was I supposed to know? I just did it by myself. The next day I left the hospital.

After I had my baby, I went back to Lejamani and lived with one of my sisters. Two years later I got pregnant again.

It's very recent that women have started taking pills and things to keep from getting pregnant. When I was young there was nothing like that. We just got pregnant and had our children.

We were taught that women should have as many children as they can. And we were also taught that when a woman gets pregnant it's her responsibility, not the man's, because she let him touch her. If the man didn't want to marry the woman or help support the child, there wasn't anything the woman could do about it.

When I got pregnant the second time, I didn't bother going to a hospital. I just had the baby at home. I suppose I'm lucky that all my births have been easy; I never had any problems. I've heard the doctors say that when you're pregnant it's good to get exercise so that the child doesn't stick to your stomach. I think that's true, because with all my children I worked and worked until the last minute—washing clothes, ironing, baking bread, grinding corn, making cheese. My stomach would be tremendous. But when it came time to give birth, one big push and whoosh—they'd come out.

The father of my second child didn't have a job, and he wasn't faithful to me either. On top of that he tried to boss me around. So I decided to raise the child by myself.

The father of my third child was no better. As soon as he found out I was pregnant, he left. So many men in Honduras are like that. They stay with a woman just long enough to have a child, then they disappear and don't do anything to help support the children. They usually don't even admit that the children are theirs.

After my third child, I went to work in the capital as a maid so I could support my children. They stayed behind with my mother. By that time my mother was living on her own, and she wanted the children to keep her company. I earned $15 a month and I sent all the money home.

This time the people I worked for didn't treat me very well. They were always yelling at me for something—that I didn't cook the food right, that I burned a pot, that I broke a dish. If I broke something, they'd take it out of my salary. I'd get so nervous whenever mealtime came around, because I knew they'd yell at me for one thing or another.

Part of my job was feeding their big dog. You should've seen the food that dog got! Sometimes he got the leftovers, but sometimes I'd make a special meal for him. My boss would give me meat, tomatoes, and oil and tell me to cook it up for the dog.

And every time I fed that dog, I'd think of my own children. My children never got to eat meat. The $15 a month I sent them was hardly enough to buy beans and corn. But that dog got meat almost every day.

I wasn't allowed to eat the same food the family ate. I'd get beans, tortillas, and rice. The family would eat in a beautiful, big dining room, and I'd eat in the kitchen with the dog. So sometimes I'd steal the dog's food. I knew he wasn't about to say anything, so I'd swap dishes with him. But I always wished I could wrap the food up and somehow get it to my children.

I only got time off to visit my children every three months. I'd leave early on Saturday and return Sunday night so I could be back at work on Monday. Aside from that one weekend every three months, the rest of the time I never had a fixed day off—only when they felt like giving it to me.

I stayed there for two years. Then I returned home to Lejamani.

It was there that I met Alberto and we started living together. I left my children with my mother because she wanted to keep them. But a few months after Alberto and I started living together, the children told me they wanted to come live with us.

I was delighted. But a few days after they arrived, Alberto started fighting with them. He wouldn't give them food. "Let them go back to your mother's house," he told me, "because I'm not about to feed another man's children." What could I do? I had to send them back.

Even while they were living with my mother, they'd come to see me during the day when Alberto wasn't around. I'd give them whatever I had—a tortilla, a piece of bread. I remember one day the oldest boy was sitting at the table eating a tortilla when he heard Alberto come in. He grabbed the tortilla, stuffed it in his shirt, and ran out of the house. I felt awful.

"Look what you've done," I yelled at Alberto. "I can't even give my own children a scrap of food. They're terrified of you. I work my ass off trying to make a few pennies to support my children, and you have no right to stop me from feeding them."

That was when I started having my doubts about living with Alberto. But I was pregnant again, and had nowhere to go.

Alberto and I had three children together. While he worked out in the fields, I stayed in the house taking care of the children, cleaning, making bread to sell, collecting milk from the landowners to make cheese—anything to earn a few pennies.

Part of the time we were happy together, but Alberto had the same problem my father did—he liked to drink. So while I scraped and saved to buy food for the children, he would spend his money on booze. But at least he didn't hit me like my father hit my mother, and he was good to his own children. That's why I stayed with him.

"The church wanted us to give out food to malnourished children, but they didn't want us to question why they were malnourished to begin with."

Malnourished ward in hospital, Tegucigalpa.

2

The Church Opened Our Eyes

After I'd been living with Alberto for 15 years, I began to work with the mothers' clubs that the Catholic church was organizing. At the meetings we'd talk about our problems and try to help each other out. We also did practical things like distribute food to malnourished children, grow gardens, and go to talks about food and nutrition. And we'd pray together, too.

At first Alberto didn't want me going to the meetings at the church, but I refused to listen. "I have every right to go out," I told him. "I'm not doing anything bad like you're doing— going out to get drunk and spending the little money we have. I'm trying to do something good."

I loved going to the meetings. It became the high point of my week, because it was a chance to get together with other women and talk about the problems we had in common—like how to keep our children fed and our husbands sober. We learned that we had rights just like men did. We learned that we had to stop being so passive and start sticking up for our rights.

I became very active in the club and was elected president. About a year later, the church invited me to a week-long course for social workers. They invited 15 women, and at the end of the course they were going to choose five women who'd be paid by the church to travel all around the area organizing more mothers' clubs.

Of course Alberto didn't want me to go to the course. I'd never been away from the house since we started living together. But I was determined to go, and I wasn't about to let him stop me. "I love you," I told him, "but I've changed. I know I have responsibilities as your wife, but I also have a responsibility to the church and the mothers' clubs."

"Now that you have your meetings and your courses, you're not the same woman you used to be," he complained. It was true, I wasn't the same. Now when he came home drunk, I'd put up a stink. I was more independent, too, since I had my own group of friends. And my work in the club made me feel important; it made me feel like I really had something to contribute to the community.

"That's right," I told Alberto. "I have changed. Before I was stupid; now I'm not the idiot I used to be. But that doesn't mean I don't want to be your wife any more. I just want things to be different."

"Yeah," he said, "now you want to be running around all over the country instead of being home where you belong."

"I'm just going to Comayagua," I told him. "I'll be locked up in the church, taking a course. It's not like I'm going to be hanging out in the street like you do. And don't worry," I joked, "what I have is all yours. No one's going to take that away from you." But he wasn't very amused. He still didn't like the idea.

I got a friend to come and watch the children. The day the course started I said to Alberto, "OK, I'm going away for a week. If you want to stay and watch the kids, then stay. If you want to go away, then go. It's your choice." He decided to stay.

I was so happy when I got to the church. I'd never been to a course before, and I was eager to learn. They read the roster: so-and-so, present; so-and-so, present. And when they said "Elvia Alvarado" and I said "present," I was so proud. So were the other women. Everyone they invited had come—all 15 of us. I'm sure they all had problems like I had, but we all made it.

We worked in groups—three groups of five each. We were all nervous, because we felt so stupid. Most of us didn't even know how to read and write. But the teachers tried to put us at ease. They said it didn't matter how much formal schooling we had, that we all had lots of practical knowledge and we all had something to offer. They said we were there to learn together, and that everyone should speak up and say what was on their mind.

Our first assignment was to look at the reality of Honduran campesinas—what we did in our homes, what problems we had. At first the women were scared to say anything. I was one of the bravest. "Elvia, Elvia," they said to me. "What should we say?"

"Don't be so shy," I said. "Don't you know what we do at home? Whatever we really do, that's what we say. And the one who writes the best will put it down on paper."

We worked hard all week, talking about our experiences as women and mothers. We talked about the most serious problems in our communities—the lack of good drinking water, no health clinic, no transportation, things like that. And we talked about how we could solve some of these problems.

It was something completely new for us. We never really discussed all these community problems, and we surely never felt that we could do anything about them. But just talking about it together made us feel like yes, maybe we could do something to make our lives a little easier.

At the end of the course, it was time to pick the five best students, the ones that would go on to organize women in other areas. I know it was hard for the teachers to pick just five of us. We'd all become good friends, and we were all full of enthusiasm. But we understood that the church didn't have enough money to pay all of us.

When they were about to call the names of the best students, I suddenly got very nervous. I saw that it was my chance to do something different with my life, to do something good for myself and other women. The mothers' clubs had opened my eyes to another world, a world where people got together and tried to change things. I wanted to take what I had learned and share it with others.

I must have been lost in thought when they called the names out, because before I knew it everyone was congratulating me. I had been the first one picked.

They divided the five of us up by sector. I was to cover La Libertad, up in the mountains. I was supposed to visit all these small communities—La Candelaria, Campo Dos, El Indio, Valle Sucio, Lajas, La Colmena. I'd never even heard of any of them before.

Our main job was to organize the women so we could distribute food to the most malnourished children. First we had to make a list of all the young children and their ages, whether or not they were breast-fed, and which women were pregnant. Then we were supposed to help them set up a feeding program.

The church organizers made a schedule for each of us—how many communities we were to visit, how many days in each place. Because you can't just go for one day and expect the women to say, "Here we are, all organized and waiting for you to tell us what to do." No, you have to spend at least three days in each community, convincing the women to get together. At that time there were no women's organizations. It was a completely new idea. Besides that, the region I was supposed to cover was far away, and the villages were hard to get to. We figured it would take me a month.

Well, of course the first thing I thought of was how the hell I could leave Alberto and the kids for such a long time. I didn't mind leaving Alberto, but I did worry about the kids. I was about to tell the church people that I couldn't do it, that I hadn't realized it meant being away from home so much. But one of the other women convinced me not to pull out.

"Look," she said, "your children aren't babies any more. They're old enough to take care of themselves. And the work we're going to do is really for them. Just think. In the future, when your children are all grown, they're the ones who will benefit from these organizations we're setting up. They're the ones whose lives will be changed."

I agreed with what she said, and decided to take the job. But I sure didn't look forward to going home and trying to convince Alberto.

Well, you can imagine Alberto's reaction when I told him I had to leave the house for a month! He hit the roof. He said no, that I had to stay home and take care of the children. I insisted I had an obligation to the church that I had to fulfill. But the fighting between me and Alberto about my work never stopped.

I left the children with Alberto and the same friend that looked after them the first time I was gone. The church paid me $75 a month. But out of that I had to pay my transportation and food, so I didn't have much left for the kids, and that was a problem.

I loved the work. I'd go from village to village organizing the women, setting up feeding programs. And we didn't stop there. We planted gardens; we even got construction materials and started building roads. You see the nice roads we have in this village? Some of them we built ourselves through the mothers' clubs. Together with the other women organizers, we set up a tremendous women's organization throughout Comayagua.

But every time I'd come home after being away from the house for a few days, Alberto would start fighting with me again. He would say that I wasn't really working, that I was out sleeping with all the campesinos. He'd tell me to wash myself before I got into bed with him.

I'd say, "Look, if you don't want to sleep with me, don't do me any favors. But don't accuse me of sleeping with other men, because you know that's not true."

On top of all that, I'd still have to put up with his drinking. I'd call him a drunk, and he'd call me a communist because I was organizing the women. The worst part was that he'd come home drunk and start throwing things around and try to hit me.

Finally I got fed up and said to him, "I'm sorry. I've been living with you for 18 years, and I really don't want to lose you. I don't want my children to grow up without a father. But you're making life impossible for me. I'm not going to stop my work, because I'm convinced that we Hondurans must do something for this country. And if you can't accept that, then you'll just have to leave."

Well, he refused to leave. He was really attached to me, since he was used to having me do everything for him. So finally I said, "*Calabaza, calabaza, cada uno para su casa,*" which is our way of saying, You go your way, and I'll go mine. I took the children and moved out of the house.

For years we moved from place to place, living with friends and relatives. It was very hard for the kids. But last year we finally got our own house. After so many years of floating around, it's like heaven to have a place of our own.

I can't say I enjoy being single. I must admit I get the desire to be with a man. "Elvia," my friends say to me, "it's not good for you to be without a man for so many years. It's not right to deny your body that pleasure." And I'm no spring chicken. But when I get dressed up to go out, I still look pretty good. Good enough for the men to come after me.

But I've taken a hard look at my life; I've looked at the relationships I've had with men. And I realize that I could never again live with a man who didn't share my values, who didn't have the same Christian principles, who didn't have the same devotion to the campesino struggle. The struggle is my life, and I could only share my bed with a man who shared the other parts of my life as well.

Many of the men who are involved in the struggle still want their wives to stay at home. They don't want their women to be active. So I've got a tall order to fill—to find a man who's not only sensitive to the campesino struggle but to the women's struggle as well!

I still thank the church for having opened my eyes. Working with the mothers' clubs, I learned how important we women are and how important it was for us to get organized.

Those of us who were the main organizers were being paid by the Catholic church. We didn't get much money, but it was enough to keep us going. We managed to set up dozens of mothers' clubs. The women were well organized, and were taking on all sorts of activities.

Then all of a sudden the church pulled the rug out from under us. It stopped the program and took away all the funds.

Why? They said there was no more money, but we don't think that's what happened. We think they were afraid of how far we'd gone.

It was the church that first started organizing us women. I'd never done anything before getting involved in the mothers' clubs. The church forged the path for us, but they wanted us to follow behind. And when we started to walk ahead of them, when we started to open new paths ourselves, they tried to stop us. They decided that maybe organizing the women wasn't such a good idea after all.

They wanted us to give food out to malnourished mothers and children, but they didn't want us to question why we were malnourished to begin with. They wanted us to grow vegetables on the tiny plots around our houses, but they didn't want us to question why we didn't have enough land to feed ourselves.

But once we started getting together and talking to each other, we started asking these questions.

We came to the conclusion that there were three classes in Honduras: the upper, the middle, and the lower class. The upper class are the rich people—the landowners, the factory owners, the politicians. They're the ones that have the power. The middle class are the workers in the city. They don't have as much money or power, but they're better off than we are. We're at the bottom of the ladder, especially the campesina women. Because not only are we exploited by the other classes, but by men as well.

So we started talking about the need for some changes. And then the very same church that organized us, the same church that opened our eyes, suddenly began to criticize us, calling us communists and Marxists. It was at this point that the church abandoned us.

W e didn't know what to do when the church pulled out. We were well organized and had begun to see some gains from our efforts. We didn't want the work to fall apart.

So we gathered together the 36 leaders of all the women's groups to figure out what to do. We agreed that the work of organizing campesina women was too important to drop. We already had this functioning organization and we didn't want to see it fall apart. So each group reported how much money it had saved, and we decided to join all our savings and give the organization a new name—the Federation of Campesina Women, or FEHMUC. That was in 1977.

The leaders went back to their clubs to explain to the women that although the church would no longer support the mothers' clubs, we Honduran women now had our own organization, run and directed by us.

I worked many years with FEHMUC, setting up cooperatives, trying to raise women's income. But I still kept coming up against what I thought was our biggest obstacle: the fact that we campesinos didn't have land to grow our food on. Most of us didn't have any land; some families had small plots but not big enough to feed themselves. I felt that without land we'd never get out of our poverty. I also knew some of the other campesino organizations, the ones the men were in, were trying to regain land for the poor. I decided to join the UNC (the National Campesino Union) and later the CNTC (National Congress of Rural Workers) so I could participate in the struggle for land.

"Most campesinos don't have houses. They have ranchos, which are made of bamboo, sugar cane, or corn stalks."

3

The Real Honduras Is Hidden

If you visit Honduras and just drive along the main highway, you might think Honduras is a rich country. The road is all smooth and paved, and the people who live alongside the highway look pretty well off. But most Hondurans are campesinos who live far removed from the highway. They live in what we call *asentamientos*, or settlements. These are villages that are not even connected to the highway by a road. Oftentimes the only way to get to these asentamientos is by horse or hiking on foot. So the real Honduras is hidden from view, but for most campesinos it's the only reality we know.

For the campesinos in the asentamientos, it's hard to make a living. If they have any land at all, it's usually the worst land—hilly with poor soils. Because the best land is the flat land the big landowners own.

The campesinos who have land of their own plant corn and beans for their families to eat. When harvest time comes, they put part of the crop aside and sell the rest. They need money to buy things like clothing, medicine, and any food they don't grow themselves.

Whenever there's a family crisis, they have to sell off part of their food to get cash. So they often run out of beans and corn to eat and have to go into town and buy them at the marketplace—for double the price they sold them for. The campesinos are always selling cheap and buying dear. That's why they never get ahead.

The guys with the fat wallets, the middlemen, come into the village and buy the campesinos' crops for next to nothing. But the campesinos need the money and have no choice. Who else can they sell to? How can they get their crops to market? There are no roads to their villages, no buses that stop there. The only transportation is their mules and their own backs.

Campesinos who don't have land are even worse off. They work as day laborers, either for a landowner or for another campesino who needs help. The daily wage in the country-side is $1.50 to $2.50 a day. But even with these low wages, they can't find enough work.

Many campesinos are forced to migrate in search of work. When it's time to harvest coffee, they go to the mountains where the coffee is. They stay for a few months. Sometimes they take their families along so everyone can help. Some-times the men go alone. In the south there used to be temporary work in the cotton fields, but no one seems to grow cotton any more.

There also used to be more work on the banana planta-tions, but they use so many machines nowadays that there's hardly any jobs for the campesinos any more. Now they have planes to spray the fields with pesticides. I think they even have machines to cut the bananas from the trees. So not only do the banana companies take land from the campesinos to grow the bananas, but with all their fancy equipment they don't even give us jobs.

The campesinos in the asentamientos don't have houses. They have what we call *ranchos*, which are made of bamboo or sugar cane or corn stalks. The roof is made of leaves and sugar cane, sewn together tightly to keep the water out.

The ranchos are just one big room, with dirt floors. Some have wood doors, others don't have any. At least they don't have to worry about locks or anything like that, because there's really nothing to steal.

The room is divided by pieces of cloth hung from the ceiling. One part is the kitchen, where the stove is. The other part is the bed for the parents, and then there's a separate section where the children sleep.

The campesinos either sleep in beds made of wood, covered with a thin mat, or they sleep in hammocks. Some sleep on a mat on the floor. They don't have sheets, just a blanket or a quilt made out of rags.

The only other furniture is a table and chairs. The campesinos make the tables themselves. And if they can't afford chairs, they sit on tree stumps.

They don't have bathrooms or running water. The women fetch the water for cooking and cleaning. They bathe in the river or stream.

In the towns, life is completely different. There are schools and stores. The houses are better—they have cement floors and tiled roofs. Many have two or three rooms, with a separate kitchen. Some have electricity and running water. But in the asentamientos there's nothing like that.

The campesinos live on tortillas and beans—three times a day, every day. When we have the money, we buy other things like rice, sugar, coffee, and cooking oil. Sometimes eggs. Those of us who live in the valleys can't raise our own chickens, because there's a disease that kills them all off. Only women that live higher up can raise chickens.

We don't have money to buy milk or meat or anything expensive like that. We buy cheese sometimes, because you can buy it in small amounts—ten or twenty cents' worth. And once in a while we buy bread at two and a half cents a roll.

We know what a good diet is. We know that a good diet has all sorts of things in it—milk, eggs, meat, vegetables. But we poor people can't afford those things. A bottle of milk costs 30 or 40 cents. With that money we could buy enough tortillas to feed the whole family.

The woman does all the cooking. When the man gets home, he eats by himself or with the children. The woman eats later.

We don't sit down to meals together like the rich people do. We don't have a special time to eat, either. We just eat when we're hungry. Not like the rich people who wait for 12 o'clock and all sit down together to enjoy this great banquet. Since we don't have much to eat, we don't make a big ceremony about it.

We don't use forks and spoons and knives like the rich; we use our fingers. The food tastes better that way. A fork doesn't have any flavor—it's just a piece of metal. And you can poke your mouth with a fork or knife. That's why we like our fingers better.

When I go to the city and eat in the market, they serve me with a fork and knife. But I just use my fingers, and I lick them clean. Sometimes the people in the city look at me funny when I'm licking my fingers. But who cares, as long as the food tastes good!

The other main expense we have is clothing. To buy clothes, the women save and save and save—penny by penny. For example, a woman goes to the market to sell a few avocados, and with her earnings she saves up to buy a used shirt for her son or a dress for her daughter. The man buys his own clothing. The woman buys for herself and her children.

We usually buy second-hand clothes at the market. I have no idea where the clothes come from. All I know is that they're cheaper than new ones. We used to buy material and take it to a seamstress. But the material has gotten so expensive, and the seamstresses charge an arm and a leg. A piece of material for a man's pants costs about ten dollars. And then another four or five dollars to have them made. It's cheaper to buy used clothes.

Sometimes we get donations of clothes from the United States, through groups like Catholic Relief Services. Last year I got two big packages of clothes from them and took them to the villages to divide them among the poorest campesinos. But with so many people in need, it doesn't go very far.

As the clothes get worn, the women sew them and sew them and sew them. You should see some of the clothing the campesinos wear. They look like a bunch of patches held together by threads.

I know campesinos that don't even have a change of clothing. When their clothes are dirty, the woman takes her children to the river to wash. They have to wait until the clothes are dry again so they can put them on and go back home.

We don't have closets or drawers like rich people do. We put our clothes in a cardboard box or hang them on the wall.

The women or their daughters wash the clothes. The only time that men do their own wash is when they're in the army. I've heard that there are machines to wash clothes. I heard the gringos on the base in Palmerola have those machines, but I've never seen one.

For the campesinos who live in the asentamientos it's hard to see a doctor, because there are no clinics nearby. When they're very sick, they have to go to the hospital in town. But since there are often no roads to their communities, the neighbors have to carry the sick to the road by hammock. Then they have to wait for a bus to town. So by the time they get there, it may be too late.

They also have a hard time getting their children to the doctor. They have to get up at the crack of dawn to get to the clinic before 7 a.m. Then they stand in line till 8 a.m., when the nurses start making the list. At about 11 the doctor begins to see patients. The worst thing is that you wait and wait, and you might not even get to see the doctor. It depends on how many people are there and what kind of mood the nurse is in. Sometimes you have to beg to be seen.

In one of the communities I visited last week, the woman left her house at 4 a.m. and carried her sick child for miles and miles. By the time she got to the clinic they told her all the appointments for the day were taken, and she should come back tomorrow! That's the kind of treatment the campesinos get. No wonder so many of our children die.

Some of the villages have rural clinics that are staffed by nurses. The nurses aren't very well trained, and they're not always there either. In one of the communities I work in, the clinic has been closed for the past six months because there hasn't been anyone to staff it.

Whether you go to the hospital or a clinic, you pay 50 cents for the visit and then maybe another 50 cents for bus fare to get there. That might not sound like a lot to you, but it can mean a choice between feeding your whole family or taking your sick child to the doctor.

Another problem is the lack of medicine. The clinics are supposed to give you medicine free, but they often don't have the right medicine in stock. So you have to go buy it in the pharmacy—if you have the money.

The worst diseases our children get are diarrhea, measles, chicken pox, fever, vomiting, and of course, malnutrition.

Measles are very dangerous. They appear in summer, when it's really hot out. If the bumps just stay on the outside, it's not as dangerous. But if they get inside the children, the children get fever and turn bright red. Lots of our children die from measles.

The children get diarrhea when they're teething, or they get it from drinking water that isn't boiled. When the diarrhea isn't too bad, we stop giving them milk—just rice water—and we buy some pills in the store. If that doesn't help, we take them to the doctor and they get antibiotics. But by the time they get rid of the diarrhea, they're usually all thin and sad looking.

Look at my granddaughter. She's a year old and has diarrhea right now. My daughter took her to the doctor, but the medicine they gave her only made the child sicker. Now they say she has second-degree malnutrition, and that we have to feed her healthier food—eggs and milk and things like that. But where are we supposed to get the money for those foods?

In the adults, there's a lot of tuberculosis and diabetes. The ones that get tuberculosis get all thin—pure bones—and they cough and cough. And the ones with diabetes get yellow and their stomachs bloat up.

We also have a lot of cancer. The doctors say that smoking gives cancer. But here the men smoke more than women, and women get more cancer. So I don't know how that can be.

The worst problem women have is anemia. Almost all the campesinas are anemic. I don't know if it's because we have so many children, or because we don't have a good diet, or what. But anemia makes women feel tired and weak.

The rich have it easier when they get sick, because as soon as they start feeling bad they run to the doctor. The doctor gets the tests right away, and poof—they get medicine and they're all better. But by the time the poor get treated they're already so sick that it's harder to cure them.

The rich can also go outside Honduras to get treated. They go to Costa Rica or to the United States. Like the former president, Suazo Córdova. They say he has diabetes and that every once in a while he goes to the United States to get his blood changed.

The most basic health problem we have is the water. The water we have isn't safe to drink. In the countryside, the people drink water wherever they can get it—whether or not it's safe. Sometimes there are even snakes in the water, and frogs. Those are things they can see. But what about the things they can't see? Because it's those invisible things, those parasites, that get us sick. It's the parasites that give our children those big, bloated bellies.

Another big health problem is flies and mosquitoes. After it rains a lot, that's when the flies come out and when everyone gets sick. Because the flies carry lots of diseases.

Sometimes the mosquitoes drive us crazy. Some nights when I stay in the campesino communities I can't sleep all night because of the mosquitoes. They're everywhere! We build smoke fires to keep them away. But as soon as the fires die out, the mosquitoes are back again. But the worst thing about mosquitoes is that they give malaria. A lot of the campesinos suffer from malaria.

The government really doesn't do anything to make the campesino's life any easier. It doesn't improve the clinics or open new ones in remote villages. It doesn't check to see if our water is safe. It doesn't make transportation any easier. The government only does things in the towns or the city, not in the remote areas where the people really need help.

Look at the roads. The government puts lots of money into fixing roads, but only when the roads lead to the homes of the rich, or to military bases, or to the border with Nicaragua.

But where the campesinos live, there are only dirt roads full of potholes. Every four years when the presidential candidates are campaigning, they pour a truckload of dirt and pebbles on the roads so their cars can get through. They do it for their own selfish interests—so they can get to the campesinos and ask for their votes—not because they're really concerned about improving the campesinos' lives.

The world of the rich is completely different. You should see the mansions they live in! We don't even call them houses—we live in houses, they live in mansions. The only poor people you see are the maids who clean their houses and take care of their children.

When I have to go to the rich neighborhoods, I get terrified, because there are all these armed guards around and you get the impression they don't even want you walking on their sidewalks. You should see how these soldiers swarm around the U.S. embassy, their rifles ready for action.

One day I had to go into one of those fancy hotels in the capital, the Honduras Maya, to leave a message for a lawyer. I was terrified to go in. I was afraid they'd stop me at the door and say, "Sorry, but you're not allowed in. It's for rich people only."

I got up my courage and went in anyway. It was like being in a foreign country, because it's not the Honduras I know. I didn't see people like me, Indians—only gringos and other foreigners, or rich Hondurans. There were a lot of fat people with blond hair.

I found out that one night in that hotel costs 80 dollars. Eighty dollars just for sleeping! I couldn't believe it. Who the hell can pay that kind of money? That's what a campesino earns in two months! I was dying to see what one of those rooms looked like, so I could find out what kind of bed you get for 80 dollars.

I looked outside and saw this beautiful pool, with the gringo children laughing and splashing around in the water. It was hot out, but they were nice and cool. They were having a great time playing in the water. And I wondered, "When will our children ever have a chance to splash around in a pool like that?" It hurts to think that I can't even give my grandchildren a decent meal, while these blond children have everything.

I always look at the children of the rich. They have rooms full of toys, while our children play with old cans and sticks. And their children are so healthy, so full of life. They're so much more active than our children are. I say to myself, "Could it be that we Indians are idiots?" But no, I think their children are smarter because they're better fed and better educated, not because they were born that way.

I want my grandchildren to have the same chances that those children do. Why shouldn't our children have toys? Why shouldn't they be well fed? Why shouldn't they go to good schools and get smart?

We're fighting so that we, too, can share our nation's wealth. We're fighting so that we, too, can live well. We all want to have good houses—with cement floors instead of dirt, with running water to take a shower and clean water to drink. We all want electricity so we don't have to ruin our eyes with those gas lights we use. We all want real bathrooms, with toilets that flush and sinks that have running water. Of course we want those things. Aren't we human beings? Don't we have the same rights that rich people do?

Why should there be rich people that have more than they need and poor who don't have anything? God didn't plan it that way. He planned for us to be equals. That's why we have to build a society where everyone has the right to live a decent life.

I know I'm not going to see it in my lifetime, and I know it's too late already for my own children. But I'm fighting for my grandchildren. I'm fighting so that one day they, too, can enjoy all the wonderful things this world has to offer.

Maybe it sounds like I have my head in the clouds. But I've heard about these astronauts in the United States who've gone into outer space. And I figure, hell, if these astronauts can get to the moon, then why can't ordinary folks like us learn to share the earth?

"I don't think God says, 'Go to church and pray all day and everything will be fine.' No. For me God says, 'Go out and make the changes that need to be made, and I'll be there to help you.' "

4

Jesus Was an Organizer

I was brought up Catholic, and I go to mass every Sunday when I'm home. I like to listen to the sermons. And when they're celebrating mass in one of the communities I'm visiting, I always go in and listen. I even listen to the people preaching in the street, because they're speaking in the name of the Lord.

Here we baptize children when they're a few months old. When we can, we dress them up pretty in a white dress. Even the boys get dressed up that way, if the parents can afford it. I was baptized and so were all my children.

When a man and woman live together without getting married, in what we call a "free union," the Catholic church says they live in sin. They can't go to confession because they can't receive the host if they're living in sin. And if you're not married and you want to baptize your child, the two parents can't go to the church together. Only one can go with the child.

I haven't taken confession in years, from the time I was a child. That's because I was living with a man and wasn't married. So I go to the mass, but I don't take confession. My children don't confess either. The people that confess are usually the youngest and the oldest—the ones that don't do so many bad things.

My mother is very religious. She's one of those old ladies that spends her life in the church. She just prays and prays, day and night. We have a very different idea of what religion is. She doesn't understand what my work is about, why I want to make changes in the way we live. She thinks we should be thankful for the little we have and leave well enough alone. I suppose she thinks that if she prays enough, God will come down from the sky with a plate of beans for her to eat.

But I don't think that God says, "Go to church and pray all day and everything will be fine." No. For me God says, "Go out and make the changes that need to be made, and I'll be there to help you."

For me, the story of Christ proves we can make changes if we fight hard enough and if we never lose faith in what we're fighting for. Remember when Christ was captured and put on the cross with two others? One was a thief, and I can't remember what the other one was. Maybe he was a thief, too.

When they were on the cross, one of the thieves said to Christ, "Hey, I thought you were so powerful. If you're really the King of Kings, why don't you save yourself? Why don't you save the both of us?" Christ kept his head down and didn't answer him.

Then the other one said, "Hey, Christ. When you're in paradise, remember me." He was saying that Christ should remember that they'd been captured together, that they'd been tortured together. And Christ answered this one. He said, "On this very day you will be with me in paradise."

That's the same as it is today. There are plenty of poor campesinos who don't believe in our struggle. They say, "Elvia? Hah! Why should I believe in Elvia? She's just a poor campesina, a nobody. No, I believe in so-and-so, because he's got bucks. He's got a car. He has a tractor. Maybe I can get him to plow my land. He can help me, that's why I listen to him. But Elvia. Hah! What could Elvia possibly do for me?"

There's a saying that goes, "As long as the poor don't believe in each other, they will continue to be poor." And that's the truth.

All this has a long history. It's just like the life of Christ. Just like there were people who refused to believe in Christ, so there are campesinos who don't have faith. Just like they captured Christ and tortured him, so the soldiers capture and torture us. And just like Christ died for the poor, so we die for the poor. The day they kill me, I'll know that I died for a just struggle; I'll know I died like Christ did, fighting for the poor.

But not all priests read the Bible the same way. There are priests who've had it easy all their lives. They're from rich families. Their parents paid for their education. They spent lots of time in Miami, in El Salvador, in Costa Rica—living like kings while they were learning the word of God.

A lot of those priests don't give a hoot about the poor. They hardly even know that poor people exist. They are great, holy priests, and that's all that matters to them. With their booming voices, they celebrate mass and speak the great words of the Bible. But they don't even listen to what it says.

You see, the Bible talks about how Christ suffered for the poor. But these rich priests don't talk about that. They turn the Bible around; they preach just the opposite of what the Bible says. In the mass, they yell and scream about what a sin it is to touch what is not yours, and how you must have great respect for private property. And they go on and on about the Kingdom of God.

Instead of making things clear, they leave everyone in the clouds. They say the poor are poor because they were born poor. So that's their lot in life. Period. You must live your life as God gave it to you. You must live in your poor shacks, because that's what God gave you. And if you're content with what God gave you and you live your life humbly without causing trouble, you'll have your reward in heaven.

The worst of all are the politicians who use religion for their own benefit. Take our former president, Suazo Córdova. Suazo Córdova was supposedly a great Catholic. That's how he tricked the people. They thought he was like the Pope of Rome because in his speeches he talked about God, and the Lord, and the Virgin of such-and-such. And you should see the church he had built in La Paz, his hometown. What a church! It's built on top of a hill, with these smooth wide roads and lights leading up to it. But what did Suazo Córdova know about God—except the God of money? Suazo Córdova got rich in office, while the people got poorer. As the saying goes, the rich dress up as sheep.

The Catholics aren't the only ones who twist the Bible around. The Evangelicals are even worse. They're the ones that go around clapping their hands and singing. We call them believers. Excuse me if any of the people who read this book are believers, but here in Honduras those Evangelical pastors are the worst hypocrites. They just live off the people. And they go around telling the campesinos that the only thing that matters is the Lord. They tell the campesinos they shouldn't take over the landowners' land; they say it's a sin to work with the campesino groups.

Some campesinos I know became believers and then decided to leave the campesino groups they were working with. When I asked them why, they said, "We can't do this any more because now we're believers. The pastor says it's a sin to be involved in campesino groups. So we're going to devote ourselves to the Lord instead."

"Your pastor wants to talk about sin?" I asked them. "Does he tell you it's a sin to die of hunger? Does he tell you it's a sin that your children are malnourished? Does he say it's a sin that you can't give them a decent meal, decent clothes, a decent education? Does he say it's a sin for pastors to live as well as he does while his people go hungry?"

Anyway, the campesinos are free to do what they want. No one can force them to stay with the campesino groups once they become Evangelicals. But I think it's a shame what happens to these believers.

I've been talking about the priests who side with the rich. But there are also many priests, mostly the ones lower down on the ladder, who are with the poor. Their sermons are different; they're beautiful. They make the Bible come to life. They say we must love our neighbors, that we must have solidarity with our neighbors, that we must serve our neighbors, that we must serve each other. They say we should follow the path of Christ, who gave his life for the oppressed.

There are priests who have died for their work with the poor. Ivan Betancour died in the Horcones massacre in 1975. One of the campesino groups that recovered land in Comayagua is named after him. And Father Rodimiro was killed at the same time. They both worked with the poor— that's why the military killed them.

We have good relations with the priests who are sympathetic to our cause. But ever since the two priests were killed at Los Horcones, the priests don't join us in the land recoveries any more. They may support us, but they don't join in.

These priests that side with the poor have to be careful nowadays. They really can't say what they think any more, because the other priests listen carefully to everything they say. The big bishops and that Pope in Rome, they don't let these priests say what they want. And the best priests are persecuted by the military. They're accused of being communists and Marxists.

Take the example of Father Tito. I don't even know what his real name is, because we've always called him Tito, ever since he was a boy. Father Tito comes from a poor family. His family didn't live in the city; they lived in a little village in the mountains. That's why Father Tito identifies with the poor.

About three years ago there was a big uproar in Father Tito's parish. The military arrested a bunch of *celebradores de la palabra*, delegates of the word. The delegates of the word aren't priests, but religious people who lead small groups in reading and studying the Bible. Since there aren't enough priests to get out into the remote villages, the priests train these delegates to go out and carry on the teachings of the Church. But since some of the delegates also get involved in organizing the poor, the military calls them communists and tries to get rid of them.

Well, after the soldiers arrested the delegates in Father Tito's parish, they went to the church looking for Father Tito. But he escaped and sent word to the Monsignor of Tegucigalpa that the military was after him. The Monsignor sent for him and kept him in the capital. I suppose the church and the military came to some agreement, because Father Tito was later sent home.

Then about nine months ago, Father Tito was visiting some small villages along the coast. He was celebrating mass with some of the delegates of the word when the army captured him. For nothing, absolutely nothing. Only because he identifies with the poor and practices the true evangelism.

Somehow, the people in Father Tito's parish found out he'd been arrested. And they were furious, because they'd heard that the gringos from the nearby Palmerola Army Base were involved in capturing him. Rumor had it that he was picked up by Honduran soldiers in a U.S. military jeep.

The people from his parish went out into the streets. "Why did they arrest Father Tito?" they shouted. "Father Tito's no thief; he's not a murderer. He's a priest, and they have to respect him. He's not an old rag they can throw around as they please. No, he's a priest, and they must respect him."

The whole parish took to the streets. I was right there at the time, because I was working with one of the campesino groups in the area. Someone got the idea that we should all get out onto the highway. They said they'd probably take him to the base at Palmerola or to the capital. In either case they'd have to pass by.

So we ran to the highway, which is the national highway, and we put rocks across it so the cars couldn't pass. In a few minutes the highway was backed up with cars and buses and trucks.

And sure enough, soon we saw a string of army jeeps. They were sounding their sirens, wheeee, wheeee, trying to get through the traffic. And smack in the middle of the military patrol was Father Tito's car. We ran and surrounded the military cars, shouting, "Respect Father Tito. Respect Father Tito. Let Father Tito go."

The people were throwing orange peels and watermelon rinds at the military jeeps, shouting and screaming. "You'll have to kill us all first if you want to get through here with Father Tito," we shouted.

And the campesinos forced one of those big passenger buses to block the road so the soldiers couldn't pass.

When the military saw that things were getting hot, they called in on their radios to the Palmerola Base. We heard them talking to their chiefs at the base.

"OK," the soldiers told us. "Father Tito is not under arrest. He's just coming with us to answer a few questions. He's coming on his own free will, because he's not under arrest."

"No," we said. "If he isn't under arrest, then why does he have to answer any questions? What are you going to ask him, if he hasn't committed any crime?"

They insisted that they weren't going to do anything with him, and that he would be right back in his church.

So the group decided to compromise. "OK," we said. "We'll get out of the highway, but we want to go with the Father wherever you're taking him." So we got a few cars together, and a group of campesinos went along. Not all of us could go, because there weren't enough cars. So most of us stayed behind while the rest followed the Father.

We got out of the way to let them through—first Father Tito, then the military, and after them the group of campesinos shouting, "Free, free, free Father Tito. Free, free, free Father Tito."

They took him to the city and kept him there a few hours, then let him go. That's how the people saved Father Tito. But to this day they keep harassing him—watching where he goes, whom he talks to.

I don't know where in the Bible it says it's a sin to organize. What about the example of Christ, who called his neighbors together and formed the seven apostles?

Christ was a great organizer. When he saw that the people were oppressed by the Pharisees, he decided to organize them. And the people followed him—first a few, and then more and more of them.

Christ walked up and down the mountains, preaching. He didn't preach in churches. No, he preached outside, in the countryside, under a tree, anywhere. He said, "All those who listen to me, come to me. And whoever doesn't want to listen to me, don't come." He meant that those who listened to him would be saved. And the apostles followed him all around while he preached.

But Christ had enemies. Everyone who tries to liberate the people has enemies. Christ's enemies captured him because one of his apostles, Judas, was a traitor. Judas sold out. And Christ, who was wise, knew that Judas had betrayed him and that he was going to die. So he called the apostles together for dinner. Haven't you seen the picture in my house, on the wall above our table? It's the only picture we have. It's called the Last Supper, and it's when Christ announced that one of his apostles had betrayed him.

Judas, the one who sold out, later repented when he saw what they did to Christ. He repented but it was too late, because they had already killed Christ. So he took a rope and hung himself.

This sort of thing happens in our organizations. We know that there are lots of Judases among us, people willing to betray us for a few dollars. They sell their principles as if they were a sack of rice. Like the campesinos who act as spies for the landowners or the military. Or the campesino leaders who sell out to the government. That's nothing new. The example of Judas is an old one. But we have to keep the faith, like Christ did. And one day our traitors, too, will repent.

I'm not afraid of death because I know that everyone dies—they die from a fever, from a sickness. We all feel a great loss when someone we love dies. When the four campesinos died in the land recuperation, I cried and cried. And when an older person dies, someone you've been close to all your life, of course it hurts. It hurts a lot.

It's even worse when a child dies. When my daughters' two babies died, I couldn't stop thinking about them. During the night I'd dream of them. They'd come back alive in my dreams. It was terrible.

If anyone thinks that we have so many children that when one of them dies we don't feel it, that's not true. We feel the death of our children and our grandchildren just like anyone else does. We love our children just like anyone else. Whether we have one or many, it's the same hurt.

But who knows what happens when we die? Maybe it's true that we just go in the ground and that's it. Everyone talks about the Judgment Day. But they talk and talk and it never comes. So maybe the Judgment Day is right now, here on earth. Who knows?

The Bible says that the rich won't enter the Kingdom of Heaven. When the Lord was on his throne, a rich man came and asked the Lord what he would have to do to save himself. And the Lord said, "If you want to be saved, go and give away all the wealth you have. Give it to the poor. Then you can enter the Kingdom of God."

The rich man walked away, thinking and scratching his head. "Damn," he said to himself. "How can Christ tell me to give away my riches to the poor! I've been working so hard to get all this money and now he wants me to give it all away. What the hell am I going to live on?"

So the rich man returned. "Back already?" said the Lord. "Did you do what I told you to do?" "No," replied the rich man. "How am I supposed to give away the things I worked so hard to get? I can't do it." "OK, go away then," Christ said. "You won't enter into the Kingdom of God." That's why we say it's easier for a camel to pass through the eye of a needle than a rich man to enter the Kingdom of Heaven.

I feel like I know Christ because they talk about him so much in the Bible and everywhere. He was a human being who lived on the earth thousands of years ago. But I don't feel like I know God. And I must admit that sometimes I wonder if he even exists.

There's a man in the town where I live whose name is Pedro. He doesn't believe in God and he just comes right out and says it. He doesn't care what people think of him. In fact, I think he likes to piss them off.

One time we were going out hunting. He loves to hunt animals. And someone said, "It's a good day for hunting. Thank God it's not raining."

Pedro snapped back at him. "Don't be such an idiot," he said. "God doesn't exist, so don't bother thanking him for the good weather."

That made this other guy really upset. "But God does exist," he insisted. "And you shouldn't talk like that, because he hears everything you say."

"Oh yeah?" Pedro laughed. "Did God tell you that himself? When's the last time you saw him? Did he stop over at your house for a drink?"

Everyone in town talks about Pedro. They say, "Pedro doesn't believe in God. That man is worse than a communist. That man is"—what's that word? Oh yeah—"an atheist." And they say that atheists are worse than communists.

But Pedro just laughs at them. When they say he won't go to heaven he says, "Heaven? What heaven? There is no heaven. The only thing up in the sky is the clouds."

So who knows what the truth is? Sometimes I think that if God really does exist, then why hasn't he come around to spend some time with us so we can get to know him? Or why hasn't someone who's spent time with him recently come back to tell us what he's like?

I've walked so many isolated trails, all by myself with my pack on my back, walking and walking. All by myself, where the only sound was the singing of the doves or the chirping of the crickets. There were plenty of chances for God to come and talk to me about salvation or whatever he felt like talking about. There was plenty of time for him to stop me in my travels and say, "Look over here. I'm God." But nothing like that ever happened.

So sometimes I wonder whether God really exists. I don't know how the world began, or who made it or anything. Sometimes I think that maybe nobody made it; that it's just always been here.

For me what exists is a spirit. What exists is faith and hope. If I'm walking along a mountain road and I'm thirsty but there's no water around, I say, "God grant me some water so I can quench my thirst." I have faith that I'll come across a stream or a spring along the way. And with this faith and hope, I keep walking and walking and walking. And after walking for miles, I finally come upon a stream. I thank God for the water, because what kept me walking all that time was my faith and hope.

I have this same faith that God will help us win our struggle. I have this faith. And I have hope.

"Married or not married, it's the same life. It's very common for men to simply leave their wives and children and start a new family elsewhere."

5

Marriage Campesino Style

One day, early in the morning, my oldest daughter Celia came and told me, "Mommy, I'm going to the river to bathe with Chela." Chela was one of her girlfriends. She took a bucket and some soap to wash with, and she left. What I didn't know is that she had already snuck her suitcase out of the house.

When it was noon I started to get worried, because she should've been back long ago. I sent one of the other girls to see if her friend Chela was home yet, but she wasn't. "I don't know why she's taking so long," I said. "She's got chores to do here in the house, so she better get back soon." Since Celia was the oldest, she was the one that ground the corn for tortillas. When she didn't show up, I sent my daughter Clara to do the grinding.

A few hours later, Chela appeared. "Didn't you go to the river with Celia?" I asked her. "Me?" she said. "No, Celia was with Tila, not with me." Tila was another one of Celia's girlfriends.

Later on one of the boys passed by the house and said, "Left you with the birdcage but no bird, huh?" "What are you talking about?" I asked him. "What's that supposed to mean?"

"You don't know?" he laughed. "Celia's gone off with her boyfriend." "No," I said. "She went to the river with Tila."

He laughed again. Then I knew it was true.

"OK," I thought, "if she doesn't want to stay with me, then let her go. If she wants to be with a man already, that's her choice."

I was mad, because Celia was only 15 years old. Besides, she was the oldest, and I needed her to help in the house. But I knew that getting mad wouldn't do any good.

For three days she didn't show up. Then the boy's father came to the house. I was inside grinding corn. "Good morning," he said. "Come in and sit down," I told him. "I'm busy and don't have time to waste." That was to let him know that I wasn't very happy about the situation.

He said, "I came to ask your forgiveness. A father doesn't know what his son is up to. And I want to know if you want them to get married or what."

"Don't worry," I said. "It's all the same to me. If your son wanted to marry her, he wouldn't have stolen her from my house. He would've made a decent wedding. But instead of a legal marriage, he stole her. I'm not going to force him to marry her. Let them live together as long as they like, and if he gets tired of her he can send her back home."

Celia's been with him ever since.

Among campesinos, men and women hardly ever get married—legally, that is. They just live together. My older son got married in the church, because his girlfriend insisted. She wouldn't give him anything until he agreed to marry her, so what could he do? When my son got married, his wife was still a *niña*, a girl—that's what we say here in Honduras when a woman hasn't been tried out by a man yet.

You see, the boys here are really bad. If the girl is loose and will give him what he wants without getting married, why bother? But sometimes the girl says, "No, I want to get married. And if you don't marry me then nothing doing." So he tells her that he wants to marry her. But if she gives in and lets him try her out, forget the marriage. If she holds out, then if he really wants her he'll have to get married.

None of my other children got married. It's all the same to me. Married or not married, it's the same life. Married women have more rights—for example, if the husband dies all his possessions go to his wife. But us poor people, what possessions do we have? None. So what difference does it make?

The church wants us to get married. Some priests go around trying to convince couples who are living together to get married. Some people give in, but most don't.

Look at me with Alberto. We lived together for 18 years. The priest that used to come here to give mass would tell us to get married. And my mother, who's a devout Catholic and spends her life praying, told us to get married. One of my brothers even tried to convince Alberto to marry me.

At first Alberto refused. He simply said no, he didn't want to be married. But after I started working with the church and getting liberated, that's when he wanted to get married. And then I was the one who didn't want to. I wanted my freedom.

Most men don't want to get married because they say that marriage ties them down. They say that if they get married, they can't have a woman on the side. But if they don't get married, they say they're free and have the right to have two women.

We Hondurans are very respectful of the church. We say, "You don't fool around with God." So once you're married, you're married. Marriage means responsibility. Because when you get married the priest says, "So-and-so, you want this woman to be your wife?" And the man says, "Yes, I want this woman to be my wife." The woman says the same thing. And then the priest pronounces them married for the rest of their lives. So if you get married in the church then you can't get divorced.

We don't have anything like a honeymoon, either. The honeymoon is running away with a woman and sleeping out in the fields together the first night. And the next day back to work. That's the campesino's honeymoon.

When a boy decides he wants to live with a girl and she agrees, he steals her from her parents' house—just like what happened with my daughter Celia, except they usually do it at night. During the day the boy tells her that he's going to take her away that night. So she goes home and pretends to go to sleep, but she's really up waiting for him. When he gets there, she makes sure everyone is sleeping. She grabs her suitcase full of clothes and quietly sneaks out the window or out the door. Then they go out to the fields to sleep together.

In the morning they go to his parents' house. When the parents see him coming home with a girl, and the girl is carrying a suitcase, they get scared. "Oh no," say the parents, "he's got himself hitched." You see, once a boy starts going with a girl, the girl moves into his parents' house.

They accept the girl whether they like it or not. A campesino family would never reject a girl their son brings home. Never.

When the parents of the girl figure out what happened, they have to decide what to do. They can go to the boy's house and ask him to marry the girl; they can wait for the boy's parents to come to them; or, if they don't like the boy, they can take their daughter back home.

But if they take her home, a few days later the boy usually steals her again. And he keeps doing that until the girl's parents agree to let her stay with him.

The boy's parents wait about three days. If the girl's parents don't come for her, then the boy's father goes to the girl's house to make an agreement. The girl's parents might say they want them to get married, or they might say it doesn't matter to them. They might say, "Let them be free and live together as long as they love each other." That way if they want to separate they can, and they don't have to worry about getting divorced.

Alejandro was a poor campesino in one of the villages I work in. He had two wives—one was named Martina and the other Marina—and he had children with both of them.

I was close to him, because he was part of the campesino group. So I said to him, "Alejandro, you have to take a good look at your life. You can't have two women—you can barely afford to support one!" "Here the men don't support the women," he laughed. "It's the women who support the men. So having two women is better than one."

The problem was that these two women fought over him. If you ever saw Alejandro, you'd wonder what the hell they saw in him. He's a skinny little man who's nothing to look at. And besides that, he's dirt poor.

One day there was a big scandal in the village, because Martina and Marina were fighting over who would get what portion of Alejandro's corn. Marina shouted, "The corn is mine, because I fed Alejandro all the time he was working in the fields. You didn't give him anything." "That's not true," Martina shouted. "What's Alejandro's is mine!"

In front of all the neighbors, Martina jumped on Marina and started pulling her hair. Marina tore Martina's dress and pulled down her underwear. Then they started rolling around in the dirt, tearing at each other.

I was in another house at the time. The daughter of one of them ran to get me, because the women have a lot of respect for me. For the campesinos, we leaders are like authorities; they count on us to give advice and act as intermediaries.

When I got there the neighbors had already torn them apart. But they were still shouting at each other and sobbing.

"Why are you two fighting?" I asked them. "Marina, you know that Alejandro lives with Martina. And Martina, you know that Alejandro lives with Marina. If you both love him, then don't fight. Now as for the problem of the corn," I said joking around, "you have to share it like you share Alejandro—one night a meal for one, the next night for the other." And everyone started laughing, including Marina and Martina.

"But seriously," I said, "we have to discuss this problem at our next meeting. We're going to ask Alejandro what he proposes and we'll come up with a solution. The important thing is to stop fighting, because it gives a bad impression. If the rich folks find out that the women here are at each other's throats, they'll be delighted. We can't fight with each other like this. It's not good for the community."

I calmed them down and they divided the corn equally. Martina went off carrying the corn on her back, while Marina loaded her horse and went home.

Two weeks later we had a meeting of the whole village, and we discussed the problem. "Don't worry," Alejandro grinned. "I can take care of this problem. I know what these women want, and I can make them both happy." Everyone laughed.

"Look, Alejandro," I told him. "You've got to solve this problem." But there wasn't much I could do, because Alejandro had been carrying on with his two families for years. His children with Marina and Martina were all in their teens already. And for Alejandro the arrangement is great. Both women work—because he has no money to give them—and both feed him. So what could we do about it at this point, except hope that he manages to keep them both happy?

When men and women start living together, there's a tremendous double standard. Because the women have to be faithful to the men, but the men don't have to be faithful to the women. If a woman lives with one man and sleeps with another, it's a terrible scandal. Men kill their wives for sleeping with another man.

But campesino men are free to sleep with other women. They usually don't go to bordellos, because they can't afford them and because they're afraid of getting some disease. But they sleep with other campesinas who don't have husbands. Some campesinas just do it because they want to. Others get paid; but we don't consider them prostitutes, because they just do it when they need some money.

It's also very common for campesinos to simply leave their wives and children and start a new family elsewhere. I'd say that about half the women in Honduras have no husbands. The men are very irresponsible. That's part of the double standard.

There are even men who keep two families going at the same time, like Alejandro. But that usually causes lots of problems, because the women start fighting with each other.

The fighting is a lot more serious when it's a woman that's sleeping around. There was a case recently right in the hotel in San Pedro. She was a married woman who had a lover on the side. Somehow her husband found out and decided to catch her in the act.

So one day he told her he had to work that evening and would be home late. Then he took the car and pretended he left, but he was really around the corner watching.

The wife called her boyfriend and made a date in a hotel. She got all dolled up and left the house in a taxi. After she'd been in the hotel about a half hour, the husband broke down the door, found them there in bed, and shot them both.

Sometimes the men just kill the wife, because they say it's the woman's fault. A man will sleep with any woman he gets a chance to sleep with, so they say it's the woman's fault if she goes with him.

That happens in the middle and upper classes—these crimes of passion. But I haven't heard of any cases among campesinos, because we campesina women just wouldn't do that. It's not in our blood. Or maybe we're too smart, because we know our husbands would kill us.

I've heard that there are men and women who make love in all different ways, but we campesinos don't know anything about these different positions. We do it the same all the time—the man gets on the woman and goes up and down, up and down, and that's it. Sometimes the woman feels pleasure and sometimes she doesn't.

We don't have any privacy either, because our houses are usually one big room. So we have to wait until everyone is asleep and then do it very quietly. We just push down our underpants and pull them back up again.

We like to have sex, but we don't let the men see us nude. That's just how we are. As soon as girls are born, their vaginas have to be covered all the time. We never change in front of men; we even take baths with our bras, panties, and slips on. And that's how we sleep, too. Take me and Alberto. We lived together for 18 years and never once did he see me naked.

Not many campesina women use birth control. They just keep having babies, babies, and more babies. I only have six children, which might be a lot in your country but it isn't a lot here. Most campesinas have eight, ten, even twelve children.

I've thought a lot about why we have so many children, and I really don't know why. The men want their wives to have as many children as they can. And most women want a lot of children, too. They think it's only natural.

Part of the reason might be the Catholic church. Most of us are Catholics, and the church tells us that it's natural to have children and that going against nature is going against God.

We campesinas don't have abortions, either. Middle and upper class women have abortions when they don't want the child or when they're afraid of gossip because they're not married. It's illegal, but they have their ways. But the only time campesinas abort is when they're sick and lose the child by accident. We don't abort on purpose; it's not part of our culture.

I never talk about family planning in the campesino meetings. There's one campesino group, ANACH, that gets involved in family planning, because it's a government organization and the government tells it to. They go around telling the campesinos not to have so many children. But the campesinos get mad; they don't like anyone telling them that.

So our group doesn't talk about it. First of all because the campesinos say it's a personal matter, and secondly because there are plenty of other groups that teach about family planning. The church teaches people the rhythm method. The health clinic gives talks about IUDs and pills and all that stuff. And the government has programs on the radio. So we don't have to get involved in those questions.

I personally don't think it's good to have lots of children if you can't maintain them. It breaks my heart to see children suffering because their parents can't afford to feed them. So I think it's good to plan.

My daughters take birth control. I told my daughter Clara that her husband is too poor for her to have another child right now. She has one child, and I think she should wait a few years before having another one—and that's it. Two children are plenty these days.

But to tell you the truth, I don't like my daughters using that birth control, because of all the problems it causes. Those pills do a lot of harm to women here. Maybe they don't effect the gringas so much, because they're more resistant than we are. They're stronger and better fed. But not Honduran women; many of them get sick.

The worst thing we get is cancer. Here in my village six women died recently from vaginal cancer. Before we never had that kind of sickness. At least I'd never heard of it before. But now lots of my friends are dying from it. Some were using pills, others were using IUDs. My sister's in the hospital right now dying of cancer of the uterus.

I once asked a doctor friend of mine, Dr. González, if it's true that birth control causes cancer. He said they haven't been able to prove it yet, but that he was worried about the big increase in women's cancer. All the women I know are scared to death about getting cancer.

Some women think that having your tubes tied causes cancer. I did it because I had to—I had high blood pressure, and it would have been dangerous for me to have more children. But most women are afraid to do it. Other methods like the IUD give lots of infections. And you have to remember that when we get sick it's hard for us to get to a doctor. The nearest clinic is far away. And even if we could see a doctor, we can't afford to buy the medicine. I know a woman who had to pay $60 to get rid of an infection in her vagina. That's more than most of us make in a month!

It's also hard for poor women to find out if they have cancer. If a woman goes to a private doctor to get one of those exams, it ends up costing her $25. And if you go to the health center to get it free, it's a long hassle. First you have to go there to get a number. Then you go back the next day and wait in line. And even then they might not see you.

When they finally take the test, they send it to the capital and it takes months to get the results. If you really do have cancer, it keeps getting worse and you don't even know. That's why so many poor women die of cancer, and that's why we're so afraid of birth control.

A lot of this money for family planning comes from the United States. What I want to know is why the United States sends us all these birth control gadgets without sending us anything to protect us against the diseases they cause? Why don't they send any medicine to stop us from getting cancer? And if there is no medicine to stop it, then they should stop sending the birth control. How can the United States go around pushing a program without thinking it through? That's just not right.

The United States gives millions of dollars to stop Hondurans from having children. I don't understand why they're so interested in our personal lives. Some say the gringos just want to get rid of poor people. Others say that the United States sees poor people as potential guerrillas, so the fewer children they have, the fewer guerrillas. I don't know, but that's what they say.

"When campesinos organize and have a plot of land to farm, they spend the day working in the hot sun. And they don't have time for drinking any more."

6

Taming Macho Ways

When I started working with the mothers' clubs in the Catholic church, it was the first time I realized that we women work even harder than the men do.

We get up before they do to grind the corn and make tortillas and coffee for their breakfast. Then we work all day—taking care of the kids, washing the clothes, ironing, mending our husband's old rags, cleaning the house. We hike to the mountains looking for wood to cook with. We walk to the stream or the well to get water. We make lunch and bring it to the men in the field. And we often grab a hoe and help in the fields. We never sit still one minute.

It's true that there are some jobs that require a lot of strength and that women can't do as well as men. For example, when we have to clear a piece of forest, it's the men who go out with the axes and cut down the trees. Other work we consider "men's work" is chopping firewood and plowing the land with a team of oxen. These are things that men do better than women, because they're stronger. I don't know if it's a physical difference from birth, but the fact is that here in Honduras women are usually either pregnant or nursing, and that takes a lot of energy out of you.

Men may be out working during the day, but when they come home they usually don't do a thing. They want their meal to be ready, and after they eat they either lie down to rest or go out drinking. But we women keep on working—

cooking the corn and beans for the next day's meal, watching the children.

Even when we go to sleep, we don't get to rest. If the babies wake up crying, we have to go take care of them—give them the breast if they're still breast-feeding, give them medicine if they're sick. And then if our husbands want to make love, if they get the urge, then it's back to work again.

The next morning, we're up before the sun, while our husbands are still sleeping.

In some families, like the workers in the city, I've seen men help women in the house. But I've never seen it in a campesino home. Even if the man has no work and sits at home, he won't help out.

I have a friend in the city who works in a factory. If he comes home from work and the meal isn't ready—maybe his wife is busy watching the children or washing clothes—he just grabs the pots and pans and gets to work. I've seen it with my own eyes. He actually cooks the meal for the whole family. You'd never see that in a campesino house!

I don't think it's fair that the women do all the work. Maybe it's because I've been around more and I've seen other relationships. But I think that if two people get together to form a home, it should be because they love and respect each other. And that means that they should share everything.

The problem some campesina women have is even worse. Not only do their husbands refuse to help, but they don't even support the family. They don't give her money to put food on her children's plates.

When the men find work, they earn a few dollars a day. The campesino with better habits gives all his money to his wife; maybe he keeps 50 cents to buy cigarettes. The campesino with bad habits gives his wife less. If he earns $2.50, he gives her one dollar and keeps $1.50 for himself.

If the woman complains and asks why she only gets one dollar while he gets $1.50, he says, "That's none of your business. I earned the money and it's mine to spend as I please." What can the woman say? If she still complains, she's asking for a fight.

That's why so many campesina women have to work. They fatten pigs or raise chickens, bake bread or sell tortillas in the market—anything to make a few pennies to feed their children.

Some of the women are sharp, though, and get money from their husbands without them knowing.

Take my friend Zenaida. She waits until her husband is fast asleep. When she hears him snoring, she gets up very, very quietly and searches through his pants pockets. Whatever money she finds, she takes. Then she crawls back into bed while the poor man is still snoring away.

The next day he gets up, puts on his pants, and goes out to work in the field. He doesn't yet realize his money is gone. But when he comes home from work, he says, "Hey, did you take some money out of my pocket?"

"Are you crazy?" Zenaida asks. "Why would I look through your pockets?"

"You did, didn't you?" he says, still not sure.

"Why? What happened?" she asks.

"I had some money I'd been saving up to buy some clothes, and it's gone," says her husband.

"You probably lost it when you were out drinking last night," Zenaida answers. "It probably fell out of your pocket while you were drunk. Because I surely didn't take your money."

He's all upset because he lost the money. Meanwhile, Zenaida's in the kitchen, laughing with her children. "Hah. Your father says he was saving the money for clothes, but he wanted it to get drunk with. I fixed him. But don't you dare tell him, because with this money I can go to the market and buy you good things to eat." So the children keep their mouths shut.

I never did that to my husband, because I always worked. I had more money than he did. But lots of women do it. They tell me about it, and we have a good laugh. It serves the men right, we say.

Another problem women have is that their husbands often beat them. Say a campesino comes home late after drinking or sleeping with a woman he has on the side. If his wife yells at him, he hits her. Sometimes he leaves her all black and blue or with a bloody nose, a black eye, or a busted lip.

The neighbors can hear everything. But since it's a fight between the two of them, no one interferes. Unless the woman starts to yell, "Help! So-and-so's trying to kill me."

Then the neighbors come over and tell him to stop hitting the poor woman.

"No," the campesino says. "This no-good woman is yelling about things she has no right to stick her nose into. I'm the man in this family, and nobody tells me what to do."

He usually stops hitting her when the neighbors get involved. But if no one comes to help her, she wakes up the next morning all black and blue.

The woman never says what really happened. She's too embarrassed. So she says she fell down or had an accident. She doesn't even tell her friends or her own mother what happened. Because if she tells her mother, her mother says, "You knew what he was like when you went to live with him. So why did you go with him in the first place?" Or if the mother tells her to come home and live with her and she does, a few days later they get back together again and the mother's the one that looks bad.

If the woman can't take it any more, she leaves him. But even after the woman leaves, the man usually follows her and keeps harassing her.

We know it's against the law to beat someone like that, but the police don't get involved in fights between couples. They say it's none of their business. They say it's something for the man and wife to figure out by themselves.

Machismo is a historical problem. It goes back to the time of our great-grandfathers, or our great-great-grandfathers. In my mind, it's connected to the problem of drinking. Drinking is man's worst disease. When men drink, they fight with everyone. They hit their wives and children. They offend their neighbors. They lose all sense of dignity.

How are we going to stop campesinos from drinking? First of all, we know the government isn't interested in stopping it, because it's an important source of income. Every time you buy a bottle of liquor, part of that money goes to the government.

That's why the government doesn't let the campesinos make their own liquor, because the government doesn't make any money off homemade brew. So a campesino can go into town any time, day or night, spend all his money, and drink himself sick. But if he gets caught making *choruco*—that's what we call homemade spirits made from corn and sugar— they throw him in jail. The government wants the campesinos to drink, but only the liquor that they make money off of.

If we're ever going to get campesinos to stop drinking, we first have to look at why so many campesinos drink. And for that we have to look at what kind of society we have. We've built up a society that treats people like trash, a society that doesn't give people jobs, a society that doesn't give people a reason to stay sober. I think that's where this vice comes from.

I've seen what happens when campesinos organize and have a plot of land to farm. They don't have time for drinking any more, except on special occasions. They spend the day in the hot sun—plowing, planting, weeding, irrigating, cutting firewood for the house, carrying the produce to market. Most of them are very dedicated to their work and their families.

So I've noticed that once the campesinos have a purpose, once they have a way to make a living and take care of their families, they drink less. And they usually stop beating their wives, too. And I've seen that once the women get organized, they start to get their husbands in line.

I know that changing the way men and women treat each other is a long process. But if we really want to build a new society, we have to change the bad habits of the past. We can't build a new society if we are drunks, womanizers, or corrupt. No, those things have to change.

But people *can* change. I know there are many things I used to do that I don't do any more, now that I'm more educated. For example, I used to gossip and criticize other women. I used to fight over men. But I learned that gossip only destroys, it doesn't build. Criticizing my neighbors doesn't create unity. Neither does fighting over men. So I stopped doing these things.

Before, whenever I'd see the slightest thing I'd go running to my friends, "Ay, did you see so-and-so with what's-his-face?" I'd go all over town telling everyone what I saw. Now I could see a woman screwing a man in the middle of the street and I wouldn't say anything. That's her business.

If someone is in danger, then, yes, we have to get involved. For example, I heard a rumor that a landowner was out to kill one of the campesino leaders I work with. I made sure to warn the campesino so he'd be careful. That kind of rumor we tell each other—but not idle gossip.

I also used to flirt with married men, just for the fun of it and to make their wives jealous. Now I'm much more responsible, much more serious. That doesn't mean I don't joke around and have a good time. I just make it clear that we're friends.

We all have to make changes. Campesino men have to be more responsible with their women. They have to have only one woman. Because they have a hard enough time supporting one family, let alone two. Campesinos who drink have to stop drinking. And campesinos who fight with their wives have to stop fighting. Our struggle has to begin in our own homes.

"There's nothing more important than getting an education. But I'm not very happy with the kind of education the kids are getting here in Honduras."

One room elementary school in rural area.

7

I Learned to Judge
for Myself

Most campesinos, even the ones who've never been to school themselves, think that education is very important. There are parents who'll do everything to send their children to school. They say, "Education is the only inheritance I can leave my children. I'm too poor to leave them anything else, so I must leave them an education."

But sometimes they just can't afford to send their children to school. Fathers often need their sons to help them in the fields; mothers need their daughters to help around the house. And even though elementary school is free, we still have to pay for uniforms, books, and materials. If the school is far away, we have to pay for bus fare, too.

High school is even more expensive. Many of the high schools charge a monthly fee. In my town they charge $7.50 a month, which is a lot for poor people. The books and uniforms are more expensive, too. So most children, if they go to school at all, don't make it past the sixth grade.

I tried to give my daughter Lidia a good education. She was the smartest of all my children, and I wanted to send her to high school. I told her, "You know, Lidia, how poor we are. I'm going to make great sacrifices to send you to high school. You pick the career you want, and I'll do everything I can to support you. I'm getting old, and when I can't work any more, you'll support me. So study hard and make something of your life. Your sisters all have families already. You're the only one left who can get a good education."

I made tremendous sacrifices to send Lidia to school, but then she went and got pregnant. She didn't tell me she was pregnant. One of my sons found out because the fellow that did it was bragging about it. Even when I confronted her she still wouldn't confess. She kept saying "No, no, it's a lie," but I felt her stomach and noticed her breasts getting bigger.

I was so furious to see her go and ruin her life that I beat her. But it was a stupid thing to do because she was pregnant. The child was born premature and I always think it was because of the beating I gave Lidia. I don't know if that's really what happened, but every time I see my grand-daughter—she's still so tiny for her age—I feel guilty for what I did.

But I had such high hopes for Lidia. I really wanted her to make something of her life. But here in Honduras, once a girl gets pregnant she can't go to school any more. She has to quit as soon as her stomach starts to show, because they don't want the other girls to follow her bad example.

Now my oldest son wants to go back to school. He wants to study at night while he works during the day. Last year he started night school to be an agronomist. I couldn't help him at all because I was helping Lidia. But he had to stop studying because he just didn't have the money to study and support his family at the same time.

Once Lidia got pregnant, he took it out on me. "I told you you should help me, not her," he said. "I'm a man and I would've helped support you when you're old. But instead you chose Lidia. Look at all the money you wasted—for nothing." And it's true. I would've been better off sending him to school instead of Lidia. But it's too late now.

I think there's nothing more important than getting an education. But to tell you the truth, I'm not very happy about the kind of education the kids get here in Honduras.

I look at the books they use in the schools. They teach the kids all about scientific and technical stuff. That's great. Don't get me wrong. I think all that stuff is important. But they don't teach them what all that knowledge should be used for. Because it's not right to use all that knowledge just to get a good job and make lots of money. No. Knowledge should be used to make life better for those who really need it—us campesinos, the poor.

Another thing that bothers me about our education system is that it doesn't teach the kids a sense of our own history— the history of the Honduran people. Why don't the kids learn about our national heroes like Indian Lempira who fought against the Spanish, or Francisco Morazán who fought to unite all of Central America? Why don't they learn about the great banana strike of 1954 or the struggles of the campesino organizations?

A real education would give the children a sense of our history and a sense of what the present struggle is about. I had to wait until I was grown and took courses through the campesino groups, but I think children should learn these things in school.

You can get a university education these days and still not know the basics of how our society works. Through my work I meet with lots of professionals, and when I talk to some of them I wonder, "My God. Has he really been through college? How could he have studied so much and still be so stupid?"

Because to tell you the truth, some of these professionals don't know their ass from their elbow. They don't understand how our society works. They don't know about the campesino organizations or the unions. I've had students come to my house to ask me what the Agrarian Reform Law is all about, because they didn't learn about it in school.

It's taken me a long time to get where I am today. I wasn't fortunate enough to get a good education. Since I only finished second grade, I never even learned how to read and write well. When I was working as an organizer for the church, I had a chance to study some more and my writing improved. I'm still very limited. I make my marks, my scribbles, and I understand them just fine. But when I need to make something look nice so other people can read it, I get my daughter Lidia to help me.

I might not have much of a formal education, but ever since I began working as an organizer I've had a chance to take lots of courses. I've taken courses from the church, from the campesino organizations, courses at the Agrarian Reform Institute. I've even taken courses given by the Christian Democratic party. That's really where I've learned everything I know.

In the courses we learn a lot of practical things, like how to keep the books and how to organize our work. But we also analyze the reality of Honduras—how the rich live, how the poor live, and why.

Before I had a chance to take these courses, I never really understood how the world worked. I was so caught up in surviving from day to day that I never had a chance to figure out just where my problems came from.

And that's true for a lot of campesinos who haven't had the opportunities I've had. They feel the pain of suffering. They feel the wounds in their bodies, but they don't know who holds the knife or why they're bleeding. They often don't even realize that the large landowners are the source of their misery.

The campesinos with the greatest understanding are the ones who are organized, because it's through the campesino organizations that they learn. The traditional political parties aren't interested in teaching the campesinos the source of their poverty because then they'd have to admit that they, too, have been profiting from their misery. And they're not about to admit that. So it's up to us, the campesino organizations, to tell the truth.

I get a lot of my information from the radio. Since so many campesinos don't read, and newspapers are too expensive to buy every day, the radio is very important for us. I don't have my own radio, but my daughter Graciela has one and I borrow hers. I listen to the two biggest news stations, Radio América and HRN.

When I have enough money, I buy a newspaper. Or else I borrow someone else's. The best newspaper is La Tribuna, then Tiempo. I'm always going around asking to look at someone's paper, because I like to at least look at the headlines. I can't read all the articles; I don't understand everything I read, but I try.

My other source of information is talking with friends. I ask the educated people I know to explain what's happening in other countries. But I wouldn't ask just anyone, because in Honduras it's considered subversive to ask about what's happening in countries like Nicaragua or El Salvador.

I like to hear what's happening in other countries. It's important for us to know what's going on in the rest of Central America. And I also like to hear what's happening in the United States, because it all affects us here in Honduras. Because the United States is the one calling the shots in Central America.

Sometimes I listen to radio stations from other countries. When I have my daughter's radio, late at night it picks up stations from other countries. I don't really know where the stations are from, but they say very different things. I think it's good to hear a lot of different views on the world.

I don't believe everything I hear on the radio or read in the paper. For example, the other day HRN was giving the news and they had this journalist on, Irma Acosta. "Hello, hello. This is Irma Acosta reporting for HRN. Attention, attention." She's a scandalous old bag just like me. "The campesinos, today, took over the private property of Mr. So-and-so, and stole the cows from his land." And I know it wasn't true. I was there; I know the campesinos didn't steal any cows.

So when I hear things like that, I lose confidence in the press. I start to ask just who it is the journalists are talking to, just where do they get their information. Sometimes they say things that are true, and sometimes they aren't true. So you have to be careful about what you believe.

When we've recovered land, we've heard reporters say that we killed the landowner's cows, that we drove the cows off the land, that we threatened to kill the landowner, that we abused his managers, that the campesinos were armed, that the weapons came from Nicaragua, that Elvia Alvarado armed the campesinos with machine guns. We've heard all sorts of lies like these.

We usually send someone to the radio station to denounce these reports and tell the truth—that the recoveries are peaceful, that the campesinos are not armed. We tell them to be more honest in their reporting. In the case of this Irma, we told her she better stop talking bullshit or we'd denounce her for being on the side of the landowners.

We get a chance to say things on the radio once in a while. But if we want to tell our side of the story in the newspaper, we have to do it in an ad. We can't do that very often, because we don't have the money for that. The landowners, the ranchers, they have money to take out plenty of ads in the newspapers. So everyone can hear their side, but not ours.

When a journalist comes to cover a fight between a landowner and the campesinos, the landowner often pays the journalist to tell the story his way, or to just not report it. If that doesn't work, if the journalist is too decent, then the landowner can make a call to the head of the paper. So it's hard to get the truth out.

And the television, forget it. We can never get on television. We've been on the radio, because we've struggled to get that access. There are still plenty of times we've sent messages and they never read them. But the fact that we do get to say our piece once in a while shows that we've achieved something. It's hard for us, because we're afraid that if we're too loud in our denunciations the government will get back at us.

When I see how the press lies about national issues, I start to doubt what I hear about international news. For example, there's a program on the television called *Today's News*. When I'm somewhere where there's a television, I listen to the international news. And all I hear is "Ooooh, ooooh, look what's happening in Nicaragua. Ooooh, ooooh, look what's happening in Cuba. Ooooh ooooh, look what's happening in communist China. Communism this, communism that." Everyone's watching this old geezer with the microphone talking about all these horrible countries. And everyone's scared to death. But has he ever been to those countries? Does he really know what he's talking about? Who knows?

When I was younger, I used to believe everything I heard. I believed everything the educated people said, I believed everything the politicians said, I believed everything the press said. But now I take everything with a grain of salt, especially what I hear in the news. Because I might not know about other countries, but I do know about Honduras. And when I hear the lies this old geezer tells about my own country, I start wondering if what he's saying about the rest of the world is true.

So I've learned that if you want to know what's going on in the world, you should study as much as you can. You should read or listen to the news as much as you can. You should take it all in, but digest it in your own way, and judge for yourself what you think the truth is.

"You read in the paper, 'Campesinos invade such and such a piece of land.' That's not true. We don't invade land, we recover land that belongs to us by law but was invaded by the big landowners or the foreign companies."

8

Our Struggle to Recover the Land

The first Agrarian Reform Law in Honduras was started by President Ramón Villeda Morales in the early 1960s. We never called him Villeda Morales. We called him *El Pajarito Pechito Rojo*, Little Robin Redbreast, because he was from the west and there was a famous song about a robin who flew in from the west.

Anyway, El Pajarito was pretty liberal minded, and when he came to power there was more freedom for the campesinos to organize and make their demands for land. In 1961 El Pajarito created the National Agrarian Institute, INA, to be in charge of distributing land.

Meanwhile, he was trying to write up an agrarian reform law that would make it legal for poor campesinos to take over private and state land that wasn't being used. But of course the big landowners and the banana companies—Standard Fruit and United Fruit—were up in arms, because it meant they would lose a lot of land. So they pressured the politicians to water it down. By the time it passed Congress in 1962, it was so watered down it was practically worthless.

Then El Pajarito was kicked out by Osvaldo López Arellano, a general. The first thing López Arellano did was try to destroy the most outspoken campesino group at that time, FENACH, and replace it with another organization, ANACH, that was more pro-government. There was a lot of repression against the campesinos and workers when López Arellano first came to power.

López Arellano eventually handed over the government to a civilian, but that didn't last long. There was a lot of pressure from the campesinos for land, and the politicians were so busy fighting among themselves that they couldn't do anything else. So López Arellano kicked the civilians out and took over again. But this time he made a deal with the unions and the campesino groups. He won their support by promising to make reforms.

One of the first things he did when he took over in 1972 was to declare a temporary Agrarian Reform Law and then pass a final one in 1975. This is the law that's still in effect today.

The law is very clear. It says that land has to be fully used, that it has to fulfill a social function. Whether the land is private or state owned, if it's not being cultivated or it only has a few head of cattle on it, it's supposed to be turned over to the campesinos.

The National Agrarian Institute, INA, is supposed to uphold the law. It's supposed to make sure the underused land gets turned over to campesino groups. But that's not what actually happens. While the 1975 law is a good law on paper, it's not being put into practice.

This is the way the legal process works. First the campesinos look for a piece of land that isn't being used properly. Then we do our homework. We find out who the owner is, how large the plot is, how much of it is planted, what crops are being grown, if it is used for grazing, how many head of cattle it has, who owns the cattle, whose land it borders. After we study all this, if we're sure the land isn't being used properly, we make a request to INA.

Then INA sends someone to look at the land and do their own study. Sometimes the staff person takes a bribe from the landowner, and then makes up a false report. The report says the land is being well used because it has fruit trees, or because there are crops growing on it. But we get a chance to see the report. And if we know it's false, we denounce it and demand a new investigation.

If the second report still comes back false, we might go directly to the person who did it. "Hey," we say, "why did you make up that false report? You know the things it says aren't true. If you're always on the side of the big landowners, if you refuse to tell the truth, we're going to denounce you to the press. We're going to tell them you're earning two incomes, one from the agrarian institute and the other from the landowners." And if they keep making false reports, sometimes we put so much pressure on them that they get fired.

If the report comes out in favor of the campesino group, then the regional director signs the request and starts a survey of the group—how many families, how many people in each family, what ages, are they married or single, how many children are in school, how many aren't in school, the names of the parents, what income they have, what they eat, where they sleep, if they have any land—a ton of questions.

Then they do a study of the land itself. They measure it; they check what quality it is.

When that's all done, the request goes to INA's attorney. From there it goes to the head of the land distribution department. As you can imagine, this whole process takes years. But in the end, the land's supposed to be turned over to the campesinos.

That's the legal process, but we've never gotten land that way. The process just doesn't work. Either the landowner pays everyone at INA off or the request gets bogged down in so much red tape that a decision is never made. We do all the legal steps first. But when that doesn't get anywhere, the campesinos say "the hell with it" and simply take over the land.

We don't call them land takeovers or invasions. No, we call them land recoveries. You read in the paper, "Campesinos invade such and such a piece of land." That's not true. We don't invade land, we recover land that belongs to us by law but was invaded by the big landowners or the foreign companies.

They're the invaders. By what right did they take the land from our families to begin with? By what right do they hold onto the land in violation of the law? Just because they have money to bribe corrupt officials or fancy lawyers to forge their papers?

So when we fight, we're fighting to protect the 1975 Agrarian Reform Law, and to protect the rights of poor campesinos to farm a piece of land.

The first land recovery I participated in was a piece of land owned by a widow named Nicolasa. She was a large landowner, a big *latifundista*. She inherited everything she owned from her father, who was one of those men who got rich by just buying wire and then fencing in the land. He put fences, fences, and more fences wherever he could. He didn't even bother to buy the land, he just put fences around it and said it was his. So this woman inherited all the land her father had stolen from the campesinos.

The campesinos in the area met every month to try to figure out what to do. The bureaucrats at the National Agrarian Institute kept saying to come back next month, or that the request was being processed, that it was in the hands of the court, that it was in the hands of the regional office, that it was in the hands of the national office, that it was in the hands of the Agrarian Council—they kept us chasing our tails and getting nowhere.

Now spring was coming again and the campesinos still had no land to plant, and no way to feed their families. They decided that the only way to get the land was to take it over themselves.

As their union leader, I accepted their decision and agreed to join them. We set the date for the following week, in the middle of the night.

When we entered the field there were about 80 of us, all men except for me. We snuck in very quietly at 2 a.m., taking our mats so we could sleep. The next day the women and children came. The women made tortillas to eat and we all went to work—clearing the land with our machetes, turning it with our hoes, and planting corn and beans. A nearby community, a poor campesino community, helped us out by sending food.

When the landowner found out we had recovered the land, she went running to the police and the army. The next day, three cars full of security police arrived to kick us out.

"Don't be afraid," I said to the campesinos. "They're not going to kill us. Besides, there's an Agrarian Reform Law in this country that says this land should be ours."

The police said we better leave immediately or we'd all be arrested. They said they knew we were armed, which wasn't true—we had only the machetes we work with. The land-owners just spread rumors like that to make the campesinos look bad.

Anyway, we decided to leave so we wouldn't be arrested. The women put the children on their backs, the men grabbed the machetes and sleeping mats, and we took refuge in the nearby hills.

When the police had gone, we returned. Four days later, the army came. They said we were thieves for stealing land that wasn't ours, that we had to leave immediately. But we said no, we weren't going anywhere, because we had nowhere to go.

The landowner was with them, and we tried to have a civilized talk with her. We said we weren't asking for all the land, just the part that wasn't being used. We told her how we needed it so we could grow our food to feed our families. But she wouldn't listen to us.

Instead she opened the fences and sent in cattle to trample the corn and beans we planted. We planted again, and she sent in the cattle again. We came back, and so did she. Four times we planted the fields, and four times her cattle tore them up.

One day, after we'd been on the land for a few days in a row, we started to run out of food. "Let's go out in the woods and see if we can find some animals to eat, or maybe some malanga," I suggested. Malanga is a kind of tuber, like a potato, and sometimes you can find it growing wild by the creeks.

"Good idea," said Mario, one of the campesino leaders. "And while the rest of you are away, I'll go water the corn we planted yesterday." So he took four boys with him and went to water the corn.

We learned a great lesson that day, that we should never let down our guard. We'd been there a few days already without the landowner hassling us. So we thought it was all right for us to split up like that.

But Mario never made it back. While he was digging a furrow to irrigate, a shot rang out from the woods and went straight through his head. The landowner had paid someone to follow him and kill him.

The boys who were with him ran to tell the rest of us what happened. "Oh, no. Not Mario," we cried. Mario was a good leader; we all loved and respected him. We couldn't believe he was dead.

I was furious. "Let's go after those murderers," I yelled. "We can't let them get away with this!" When I get mad, there's no stopping me. I grabbed my machete and went to hunt them down. All the campesinos followed me. We didn't even stop to think that it was our machetes against their guns.

We walked throughout the woods all day long, but we never found the bastards.

Meanwhile, we'd sent word to our union leaders in the capital. By the time we returned, the head of our union was already there. He was mad as hell.

We took Mario's body to the town and held a vigil. Everyone in the community came to pray for him. His family was crying and crying. It was painful for all of us. You could hardly recognize him, because his head was all crushed.

We collected money to help the family, and after the vigil we went right back to the land. We knew that crying wouldn't get us anywhere. We had to go back to the land and refuse to leave it. We had to use his death to give us even more courage.

The campesinos grabbed whatever they could find—machetes, sticks, stones. And this time we did get some guns—old hunting rifles. Someone in the community rounded them up for us when they saw what had happened.

We charged into the landowner's house. She didn't live there; she lives in a big mansion in the city. But we threw out her managers and servants and took over the house.

Then we waited for the army or the landowner to appear. We were still mad as hell. "OK," we said. "They already killed Mario. Let them come and try to kill us all."

When the army arrived, we told them we weren't as well armed as they were, but that our bullets could still kill. We said we wouldn't open fire unless they did first. They realized they couldn't get us out without a big scandal, so they eventually left us alone.

That's how we won the piece of land those campesinos are farming today—with the sacrifice of one of our best leaders. And as for the landowner's house, we use it for our meetings and for hulling rice.

Another land recovery I led was on a piece of land belonging to the sister-in-law of ex-president Suazo Córdova. The first thing we did once we got on the land was to raise the Honduran flag and the flag of the campesino union. The campesino flag is white, red, and black. White stands for purity, red for blood, and black is a symbol of mourning for the martyrs who died in the struggle.

After we raised the flag, we began planting the fields. The next day the landowner sent a tractor to plow the land. She wanted to tear up our seeds, but she was also trying to prove to the authorities that the land was being well used, since the law says only idle land can be taken over.

We knew that if we let that tractor in, we'd lose the fight. So a few of us jumped in front of the tractor and forced the driver to stop. "You can't plow this land," we shouted. "It belongs to the campesinos now."

"The owner is paying me good money to plow this field," he answered, "and I can't waste my time talking nonsense with a bunch of campesinos."

"Well, you're not coming in," we told him. "We're the owners now, so you might as well turn around and go home." When he looked around and saw he was surrounded by hundreds of men, women, and children, I guess he changed his mind. He turned around and drove off.

We went back to work. Three days later, the landowner's three sons appeared, armed to the teeth. They had rifles and machine guns, weapons they must have gotten from their friends in the military. First they let the cattle in to trample the field, and then they started taking pot-shots at us. "Get down on your bellies," I shouted to the campesinos. "Lie flat and move along like snakes!" We slithered away as fast as we could. The boys kept firing at us, but thank God no one was hurt.

We returned after they left, but we knew the sons would be back to shoot at us again. I knew it was going to be a tough fight and that we had to be prepared for the worst. "Do you have the balls to really win this fight, or don't you?"

I asked the campesinos. They said yes, that they had no intention of turning back. So we came up with a new plan.

The next time the landowner's sons appeared, we'd be ready for them. The bravest man would stay up front with me, and the rest would be hiding behind us in five rows of ten each.

Saturday, they drove up with their rifles and machine guns. They cut down the fence to let the cattle trample our fields again. But we were hiding behind the bushes, surrounding them. I told the men, "When I wave this stick, I'll jump out. Then you all jump out behind me."

I waved the stick and jumped out, and they all followed. We captured two of the boys and tied them up. The third son, who was still in the car, went for his gun.

"If you shoot," I warned him, "your brothers are dead." He looked over at his brothers and saw the blades of the campesinos' machetes at their throats. "Go ahead," I told him. "Shoot or drop your gun." He dropped his gun and the campesinos ran and surrounded the car.

I was holding a bag with tortillas and a napkin in it, since I'd been eating my lunch when the action started. I turned around, grabbed a stick and put it in the bag. Then I jumped in front of the brother in the car, holding the bag with the stick in it as if it were a pistol.

"We're not going to kill you," I told him, waving the bag with the tortillas in front of his face. "We just want to make sure that you're going to leave us alone. That's all we want. This land now belongs to us, and we don't want you coming around to bother us any more. Now get out of here."

You should've seen how frightened he was! He really thought the stick was a gun. He didn't even look behind at his two brothers. He just zoomed out of there as fast as he could.

Then I went over to where the two brothers were tied up. "Did you check them out and make sure they're not hiding any weapons?" I asked the campesinos. "Oh, yes," the campesinos said. "We went over them real good. We even took off their boots and shook them out. They're clean."

But something bothered me. There was something about one of them that just wasn't right. He had a bulge between his legs that was too big to be real. So I looked and looked, and finally I went up to him and stuck my hand down his pants. "Let's see what you've got here," I shouted. And you know what I pulled out? A big plastic bag full of marijuana!

"Ay, Señora," he said. "The army will come and find me carrying marijuana. Can't you just bury it in the ground and not tell them?" he pleaded. He was probably afraid of what his mother would say.

"Do you think I'm stupid?," I asked him. "You want me to bury it so that you can say it's mine? No way. When the soldiers come I'll turn you in, marijuana and all."

Then we waited for the army to come. I told the campesinos not to worry if they arrested me, because the union would soon find out and would come to get me out. I explained that if I was arrested, the campesinos should hide until the soldiers left, but come back the next day. "If you get scared and don't come back," I warned them, "then we've lost the fight." In the meantime, I told them to start weeding the fields with their machetes, so that when the soldiers arrived they would find them at work.

You wouldn't believe how quickly the soldiers came. When a poor man is in trouble, they're nowhere to be found. But when a rich man needs help, they show up in no time.

Two cars full of soldiers came roaring in. Their leader, Colonel Aspra, jumped out and ran up to me. "Señora," he said, "you're the leader, aren't you?" "I'm just a poor campesina," I told him. "There are 50 campesinos here, and no one is the leader."

"Señora," he said, "don't you know that kidnapping these men and tying them up is a serious offense? And so is trying to take over land that doesn't belong to you."

"Colonel," I told him, "you can't tell us these lands don't belong to us, because you're not a representative of the National Agrarian Institute. We have no reason to talk to you about our rights under the agrarian reform. You're from the army, and all you know about is guns. You shouldn't go around sticking your nose into matters you don't know anything about."

I think he was amazed I had the nerve to talk to him like that. "We're just here to protect the law," he said.

I laughed. "If you were really here to protect the law, you'd be giving this land to the campesinos. You're not here to protect the law; you're here to protect the rich.

"If you want to arrest me for kidnapping, go ahead," I told him. "But the truth is that these boys came here to kill us, just like they did last week. We captured them to avoid a massacre. If you want to take them, go ahead. We have no reason to keep them here. And if you'd rather arrest us instead, go ahead. But be clear that we're not here because we want to cause trouble. We're here because there's an Agrarian Reform Law in this country, approved by the President of the Republic and by the military itself. And if you don't want to uphold that law, then we campesinos must do it for you. So if you want to arrest me for merely upholding the law, then go ahead."

Then I remembered the marijuana. "And you know what else?" I told the colonel. "Not only do the rich violate the Agrarian Reform Law, but they're also drug addicts." I pulled out the bag of marijuana. "You know where he was hiding this, colonel? Want to take a guess? He had it right here," I pointed to the young man's penis. "Right here between his testicles."

"Ah-ha," said the colonel. "They caught you carrying marijuana. Now you're in trouble." So we untied the two boys and the soldiers took them away. They held them in jail for two days, and gave them a stiff fine for possession of marijuana.

We campesinos had a good laugh. "You know how happy the soldiers must be with us?" I told them. "Not only did they get to pocket the big fine, but they also got to smoke the marijuana."

A few months later, the National Agrarian Institute gave the campesinos legal title to 50 acres of that land.

It's not as if we always win. There are some recoveries that just don't work. I remember one piece of land that belonged to a rich doctor. We took over that land four times, and four times they kicked us out. We finally took the case to the Agrarian Council.

The Agrarian Council is made up of government lawyers and representatives of some of the campesino groups. So sometimes we get a fair hearing. In this case we won, and the campesinos were so excited that they finally had the land.

But the doctor took the case to the Supreme Court. The cases hardly ever go to the Supreme Court; but when they do it's usually the rich who win, because they have the best lawyers. And that's what happened. We put up a good fight, but we didn't win.

And don't think that even when we do get the land titles our problems are over. No, they're just beginning.

The Agrarian Reform Law in this country is supposed to be an integral law. That means that when the campesinos get the land, they're also supposed to get credit and technical assistance. It's supposed to be a whole package. The campesinos need credit to buy seeds, to rent a tractor or oxen to plow the land, and to have something to live on until the harvest. And they need technical assistance to figure out what varieties grow best and how to market their crops.

But the truth is that if you get the land you don't get technical assistance. And if you get technical assistance then you don't get credit. There's always something missing. What good is the land without money to make it produce? What good is technical assistance if you don't have the money to buy what the agronomist advises?

For example, our campesino organization works with a group called El Carmen. This group won a piece of land; but instead of using it to grow corn and beans on, INA encouraged the campesinos to grow sugar cane and loaned them $3,000 to grow the cane.

But what happened? The Ministry of Natural Resources was supposed to give them technical assistance, because the campesinos had never grown sugar cane before and needed help. But planting time came and no one showed up to help them decide what was the best type of sugar cane for their land. So the campesinos went on their own and bought some cane to plant, but it wasn't the right kind. They didn't manage to grow enough to pay back the loan.

Other times the campesinos get the loan, but it comes too late. It arrives after planting season. So they plant late and the crops grow in the heat of the dry season. The project fails and they can't pay back the loan.

When the campesinos are in debt, it makes it harder for them to feed their families. The family needs corn and beans, but to pay back the loans they have to grow cash crops—like rice or sugar cane or watermelons—and that means less land for food.

Getting loans from INA is very complicated, because it's a government institution and there's always a lot of red tape. It's even harder to get loans for women's groups. If the women want to get credit, they have to be the wives of the men who have legal title to the land, they have to know how to read and write, and there are a whole bunch of other requirements. One women's group is trying to get $250 for a corn mill so they won't have to grind the corn by hand. They've been waiting two years for a loan from INA, and they're still waiting.

Another women's group is trying to get a consumers' store, because they have nowhere close by to buy their cooking oil, rice, soap, sugar, coffee—all the things we campesinos need. The nearest store is far away in town. They have to walk for miles just to buy a bar of soap. The prices in town are high, and the women have no transportation to carry their packages back home. So they want a store in their own community that sells the basics at cheaper prices. But we still haven't been able to get a loan from INA, because their husbands owe INA $1,500. Until the men pay back the loan, INA won't give any money to the women.

Not only do we have to fight for credit and technical assistance, but once we get the land we also have to fight for water, schools, clinics, and all the things a community needs. And we still have to deal with the landowners, who continue to harass the campesinos.

There are even cases where we've gotten the title, and INA has turned around and tried to take it away again. We have a group in La Palma that had been farming a piece of land for about eight years. They'd been farming without title to the land, and it took them eight years to finally get legal title.

But no sooner had they gotten the title than this woman came along and said the land was hers. She went with her lawyer to INA and convinced them she owned the land. So INA sent the group an eviction notice.

The group contacted me immediately. I was furious and went storming into INA. "What on earth do you think you're doing?" I asked them. "How can you give the campesinos the land and then say it belongs to someone else? Are you out of your minds? Those campesinos aren't budging."

The campesinos refused to leave, and INA still hasn't been able to get them out. But it just shows you how crazy the whole process is.

Right now I'm trying to deal with another case in La Palma where a campesino group was tricked by a mine owner. This group won a piece of land that included a limestone quarry. The campesinos mined the quarry and sold the limestone to a cement factory. But they didn't have any trucks or equipment, so it was difficult for them to make much money.

One day, a mine owner came and asked the campesinos for permission to work the mine. He said he'd give them $200 up front, and $50 a month. That was more than they were making, so they agreed.

The mine owner got a lawyer to make up the papers. Then he took the contract to the group's leaders to sign. The campesinos realized that the only thing the document talked about was the $200 up front, not the monthly payment. But the mine owner said, "Oh, that doesn't come in the contract. Don't worry, you'll get your $50 a month, but the contract is only for the initial fee."

So the trucks started coming in and taking out the lime. And the mine owner was making good money, but he never paid the campesinos the $50 a month he'd promised. He paid the first $200, that's all. For four years he worked the mines. Four years! And he didn't pay the campesinos a cent.

The bastard lived far away, and he never came to the mine himself. He just sent his workers. So the campesinos had to spend their own money trying to find him. They'd go to his house, and he'd never be there. Wherever they looked for him, he was somewhere else.

Finally the campesinos came to our organization for help. "This man cheated us," they said. "And we want to do something about it."

We told them to stop the trucks from coming in until the man paid up. So they all took their machetes and stopped the trucks. "No more," they told the drivers. "You'll have to turn around and go home. Just tell your boss you can't come in any more until he pays us the money he owes us."

Soon after that, the campesinos got a letter that on such-and-such a day, the mine owner would be there with the local judge. The campesinos asked me to be there to defend them.

The mine owner showed up with his wife and the judge, who was obviously already on their side. I told the judge that I was there to represent the group.

The judge read us the document about the $200. "Yeah," I said, "but what about the $50 a month he promised to give them? Why didn't he put that in the document?"

"Fifty dollars a month?" said the mine owner. "I never promised any such thing."

"Yes you did," the campesinos yelled. "You're lying. You said you'd pay us every month, and you've been working here for four years, making a ton of money, and you haven't paid us a cent."

The judge ordered us to let their trucks in. "No way," I said. "Their trucks aren't coming in until he pays up. If he wants to continue working here, he'll just have to add up $50 for every month he hasn't paid, and give that wad of bills to the campesinos. If not, then the hell with him."

The mine owner's wife was furious. She started yelling and screaming at me, saying that I was disrespectful, that I was was just a dirty, loud-mouthed campesina. "You have to let our tractors in," she screamed. "Those campesinos signed the papers." Her face got all red and puffy. I thought she was about to explode!

The judge got mad at me, too. He said I was inciting the campesinos, and he threatened to throw me in jail.

"Look," I said to the judge, "I'm not being disrespectful. I'm only defending the campesinos. How can this man get away with lying and cheating? He's the one that should be in jail. And if it's a crime to make a fuss, then why don't you arrest his wife? She's the one who's shouting and screaming and raising hell. You know why you don't? Because you're on the side of the mine owner. You're supposed to uphold the law, but instead you defend the rich."

The three of them got mad and left. About a week later the judge issued a warrant to arrest the three campesinos who had signed the document. The police went out looking for them, but they went into hiding. Since the police couldn't find them, they arrested another campesino instead.

"You bastard," the police said to him, sticking their rifle butts in his back, "show us where those sons-of-bitches are hiding." He wouldn't say anything, so they dragged him off to jail.

The poor campesino's still in jail. I have to go find out what they intend to do with him and how I can get a lawyer to defend him.

When you think about it, the campesino has the patience of a saint. He's deceived, cheated, and tricked, time and time again. But the campesino is patient. Look how that group at La Palma waited four years for the mine owner to keep his word! Four years!

But there comes a time when their patience wears thin. There comes a time when they get tired of being humiliated and they say, "We've been pushed around for too long. Enough is enough."

It's dangerous when the campesinos react, because their reaction is often violent. They say, "Now we'll see who's got balls. We're gonna solve this with our machetes." And when the campesinos fight, they really fight.

So one of our biggest problems is calming the campesinos when they get mad. We say, "Yes, it's true we've been cheated. It's true we've been suffering for too long. But we have to keep struggling peacefully, because if we take the violent route we'll lose everything."

Sometimes we have to calm them down, and other times we have to give them courage. When we go to recover the land, we have to keep their spirits up. The odds against us are so great that we constantly have to convince the campesinos that it's possible to win.

At the same time we have to prepare them for the worst. We tell them how the landowners pay thugs to kill the campesinos; we explain that others have died in recoveries. We make sure they understand that they have to be ready to be jailed, to be abused, to be persecuted, and if need be, to die.

And we have to be right there with them in the trenches. Otherwise they'll say, "Our leaders are worth shit." We have to show them that we're with them all the way. That's the only way we can gain their trust.

Because the land recoveries are no joke. And the only ones that get killed are the campesinos. You never hear of a landowner getting killed. That's unheard of.

But look at how the campesinos die. There's the massacre at Talanquera in 1972, where the landowner found out the day and time the campesinos planned to recover the land. When this group entered at four in the morning, the landlord's thugs were waiting for them and opened fire. Six campesinos were killed.

Then there's the massacre at Los Horcones in 1975, when one of the unions, the UNC, was staging a march on the capital to pressure the government to pass the Agrarian Reform Law. The cattle ranchers paid the military to kill the campesinos. Five demonstrators were killed at a UNC training center. Nine others—including two priests—were tortured and killed at the ranch of José Manuel Zelaya, and their mutilated bodies were found stuffed in a well.

There was another massacre on the north coast that I don't know much about. And when we recovered land from the widow Nicolasa, Mario was killed.

The campesinos don't have guns, only machetes. When I join the recoveries, I usually don't even have a machete. Maybe a knife that I use to peel oranges. What good is a knife going to do me? That's why the landowners kill us, because we can't defend ourselves. It breaks my heart to see my compañeros cut down, defenseless. And the landowner with his guns and automatic weapons.

It makes me so mad. I just get furious when I see how we campesinos die, like dogs. Our lives aren't worth a penny. When a rich man dies, a fleet of fancy cars takes him to his grave. When a campesino dies, we're lucky if we can find a few pieces of wood to make a coffin. And that hurts. It hurts bad to see a campesino die in a land recovery. I've never in my life cried like I cried when I saw our compañeros killed.

I know that the life of the poor is one of suffering, and I don't cry over that. But when I see a campesino killed, then I cry. I cry to see them die with no way to defend themselves. Like a dog.

I don't even want to remember. I don't want to remember the time the four compañeros were shot in Talanguita. Four good friends. We all went to bury them. We all had to look at the four of them in those boxes, with their heads blown to bits by the landowner's bullets. It pains me to remember those moments.

That's why I struggle and why I'll never stop struggling. Never. Because with all these campesinos who have died fighting for a stinking piece of land, how can we stop now? No. We have to fight with more courage, more conviction, more strength.

"It's often a tough battle to win the women over. But once you get them organized, they change overnight."

Women from a cooperative work on recovered land.

9

Organizing Brings Change

We campesinos have learned over the years that the only way we can protect our rights is by organizing. Actually, we learned that from the banana workers who worked for United Fruit and the other gringo companies. They started organizing for better work conditions, and in 1954 they had a big strike that spread to the banana plantations all over the country.

We also learned to organize by watching the rich. They were the first to organize, and they're the best organized. They've got their private enterprise organizations, and then they have the government and army organized to protect them. They're super organized; so if we ever want to change anything in this country, we have to be even more organized than they are.

There are four major campesino organizations—ANACH, FECORAH, the UNC, and the CNTC. (See Appendix 4.) FECORAH is in bed with the government. It doesn't even try to recover land for the campesinos. ANACH doesn't do much either; because once the recoveries started and the repression against the campesinos got worse, the leaders of ANACH panicked and started making deals with the government.

The UNC really pushed recoveries in the past. In fact it was the organization that carried out the first recoveries. It used to be the most outspoken campesino organization. But lately it, too, has begun to sell out. It started getting money from the government, and ever since then it started forgetting its purpose. That's why I switched from the UNC to the CNTC.

The CNTC was created in 1985. It's a new organization, and it's now the only one really pushing to implement the agrarian reform. There are thousands of men and women organized in our union. About half are women, and there are many women organizers like me.

The main thing we do is help the campesinos get land, credit, and technical assistance. And we help defend them against the landowners and the military.

We regional leaders help organize the groups; but once they're started, the campesinos run them on their own. We check with them to see what problems they're having and how we can help, or they come to us for advice. But each group has its own leaders who run the group on a day-to-day basis.

The groups decide on their own how often to hold elections. Some groups rotate every year, others every two years. When we choose the regional and national representatives, we use secret ballots and there are two or three candidates. But the local groups choose their leaders by consensus. And they keep rotating so everyone gets a turn.

My position in the CNTC is an elected position. I'm the financial secretary for the region of Comayagua. I ran against a man, and I won. It's a two-year position.

When my time is finished, I can run again for one more term, I can run for another office, or I can go back to working with the women's group I belong to. If I went back to the women's group, I'd work the land just like they do. Because all the leaders belong to a group in their community, and when their terms are over they go back to work there.

When elections are held at the national level, each campesino group sends a representative to the National Congress. The national leadership is elected every two years. They can be reelected for one more term, but that's all.

The regional office gets its money from two sources—from the national level and from the union dues of the campesino groups. The groups have to pay a quota if they want to be affiliated with the CNTC.

Our main problem with money is that we never have enough. But we don't have problems that other groups have of people stealing from the union funds, because everyone keeps their eyes open. At our monthly meetings we go over our finances, and all the regional leaders look at the records. The financial secretary has to give a monthly report, complete with signed receipts—receipts for the rent, notebooks, money for bus fare, everything. And since we're such a poor organization, there's really nothing to steal.

The groups at the base meet more often—every week or two—and they keep the same kind of records. Their money problems are not over stealing either, but from bad administration. Say a group takes out a loan for $2,500 from INA—but if INA doesn't give them technical assistance and the money is poorly spent, they can't pay back the loan and the group goes into debt. That's when the regional leaders step back in to see if we can get them back on the right track.

As I said, our main problem with money is not having enough. Our union doesn't get money from the government like some of the other campesino groups do. We get some outside help from groups in other countries like Europe, but the CNTC is basically an organization of poor campesinos.

The CNTC puts a lot of emphasis on organizing women. Our organization's principles are very clear: they say that women must be integrated into the agrarian reform process. So no matter how difficult, all union leaders—both men and women—must work to organize women.

All the campesino organizations say they're organizing women. All of them have a position in the leadership for "women's affairs." But what happens with most of these women's groups is that they're really created to get international funding. The foreigners love to fund "women's projects." So all the campesino groups respond by creating women's projects.

And what happens? When the project is finished, or if the project fails, the women's group disintegrates. We're not interested in organizing women around particular projects. No. We want women to organize for the sake of organizing; and out of their organizations, projects will emerge.

Some of our women's groups are also involved in the fight for land. Sometimes the women get their own piece of land and work it themselves. I have one group of women, for example, that grows watermelons together. The women also get involved in activities like setting up consumer stores or daycare centers.

I remember in the beginning how difficult it was to organize the women. First of all, it's often hard for women to understand the need to work together. It's much easier to organize the men because their problems are more obvious. They need land. And to get the land they must be organized, because INA only gives land to organized groups. As the saying goes: "The ox that's thirsty will look for water." So the campesinos who are thirsty for land are eager to get organized.

But the hardest part about organizing women was that their husbands were so opposed. The men thought that organized women would want to wear the pants in the family, that they would want to start bossing the men around. They said that men should tell women what to do, not the other way around.

There are still many women, especially in the most isolated areas, who just don't want to get involved. They say, "No, I can't leave the house. I can't leave the kids alone. I don't have time. My husband will get mad."

It's often a tough battle to win the women over. But once you do manage to get them organized, they start to change overnight. For example, when men and women are together in community meetings, the women who aren't organized are real quiet. They're afraid to speak out in front of the men.

But you should hear the organized women! Sometimes they talk even more than the men. To quiet them down the men say, "These women are good talkers. But it's all talk and no action." And the women say, "We can talk as much as we like. Everyone is free to say whatever they want." That's why the men are often afraid of the women organizing. Because once we're organized, you can't shut us up.

When we do the recoveries, the women help out. But it's hard for them, because they have to return home to make the food and take care of the children. So they're much more limited than the men are. Because you see how difficult it is here. Just to make a meal takes hours. We have to start by grinding the corn. It's not like in the city or in other countries where everything is ready. It's not like a campesina can open a can and poof—dinner's ready.

But if the men are jailed, the women take over and work the land. They stand up to the soldiers, they go to the jails to get their husbands out, they sleep out in the fields to keep the land. Were it not for the women, there are many battles the men would've lost.

It's funny. While there are men who complain about their wives being organized and out of the house, the men never complain that I'm a woman. I've never had that happen, and I don't think any of the other women organizers have either.

When the soldiers arrest the campesinos, I've heard them say, "You idiots let a woman tell you what to do? What kind of men are you?" But the campesinos never say anything like that. They have great respect for me and the other women leaders. Once you win their respect, it doesn't matter if you're a man or a woman.

The men also understand that the women organizers are compañeras in struggle but not compañeras in the bed. Our relationship is a work relationship. We're there to help them out, to work towards a change in our society, not to sleep with them.

We walk up and down the mountain trails together; we work out our problems together; and if we get caught somewhere late at night, we all sleep in the same hut together. But the men never touch the women organizers, unless of course there's a mutual understanding. The relationship between men and women in the union is always a relationship of respect.

Sometimes the women who aren't organizers find this difficult to accept. Since we spend so much time with the men, some of the campesina women get jealous.

They don't say anything to me. They tell one of their friends, but it usually gets back to me. They say they're jealous because I spend so much time with their men, and that sometimes I sleep out in the fields with them, and who knows what I'm doing with them.

So when I'm in a meeting with the women, a meeting where we discuss the women's projects, I bring it up. I say, "Look, I want to get something straight. I'm a representative of the union. I work with the men because we're fighting for land. That's why I'm here—to work, to struggle, that's all. I know that all the men have their women, all of them have their families.

"Our struggle is to unite, not to divide. I would never destroy a family. If I destroyed a family, I'd be destroying our organization. Because the women would start fighting with the men and among themselves, and the whole group would fall apart.

"So I want to make it very clear—I would never do anything bad with your men, because it would go against my principles. I'm a campesina just like the rest of you. I'm not here to cause you any harm. I'm here to help you out. And for me to do that, you must trust me."

That's how I start gaining their confidence. Because there are men who would like to sleep with me. When you spend so much time together, they start to fall in love with you. They haven't learned to control their desires. But I have. Even if I'd like to sleep with one of them, I know I can't because it would only cause problems.

It's different with the male leaders; they're freer than we women are. They have their wives at home, but some of them have women on the side. Not campesina women, but women in the city. I don't think it's right; I think a leader who has a wife at home and goes with other women is violating our principles. Because within this struggle we're waging we have to be honest, we can't be corrupt. And honesty begins in the home. If we're not honest at home, I'm not sure we can be totally honest outside the home.

Another thing about the male leaders is that they often don't want their own wives to participate. They talk a good line about "the role of women," but when it comes to their women—well, that's a different story. I've never even seen the wives of some of the leaders, they're so well hidden.

So I tell them, "Hey, you big talkers, why don't you unlock your wives and let them out of the cage? Bring them around sometime so we can make sure they really exist."

I already told you about how we organize land recoveries. But we also try all sorts of other tactics to get land and credit for the campesinos. We organize marches; we hold sit-ins, hunger strikes.

One time, about six years ago, we had about ten groups that were trying to get a piece of land. They'd done all the applications, they followed all the rules, but the regional director of INA refused to process any of our petitions. The police were also holding over a hundred campesinos for land invasions, and we couldn't get them out of jail. We talked to the judge, we talked to the police, we talked to the security forces, to the army, to the court, to the prosecutor. But we couldn't get them out.

So we decided that the only option left was to take over the INA offices.

We went in five at a time, five more, five more, five more—until there were 300 of us inside, men and women. I was in charge of watching the front doors. We had decided beforehand that when we were all in, someone would whistle and that would be the signal for me to shut the front gate. When we were all inside we closed the doors and locked the employees and the director in.

We marched into the director's office and told him that it was high time he started working for the campesinos, not the landowners. We disconnected his telephone and left a few campesinos to keep watch over him.

Then we gathered together all the secretaries. "Now you're working for us," we told them. "We're the bosses now. So get to your typewriters and type what we tell you."

We had the secretaries write communiqués for the press. And we took the telephones and called the press in the capital. Soon the military was surrounding the place, but we wouldn't let them in.

There were hundreds of us, and we were all shouting, "We want land; we want land; we want land." We didn't let anyone in. We spoke to the journalists from the gates. And when they tried to take photos, we wouldn't show our faces, only our backs. We didn't want the intelligence police, the DNI, to have a record of who was there.

The military was swarming all over. But they didn't rush in or throw tear gas, because we had the director and the employees inside.

We stayed there all day long, until about 6 p.m., when a commission from our headquarters in the capital arrived. I was still with the UNC at the time, and the head of our union was a great leader, Marcial Euseda. He and three other UNC leaders met with the regional commander, Colonel Aspra, and the head of the intelligence police.

The army told us to leave the offices, but we refused to leave until we were told to do so by our union leaders. "If Marcial says we should go, we'll go," we said. "But if he doesn't, we stay." So they let Marcial in.

He said, "Compañeros, compañeros, calm down. We're going to start negotiations with the director of INA and the military. In the meantime, you all should leave the INA offices and meet across the street in the park."

And I said, "If you're going to negotiate with those military bastards and the director of INA, then negotiate. But remember what we want: we want land for all ten groups, and we want our comrades in jail released. We'll leave the offices when the negotiations are over and we've got what we asked for. Until then we'll stay right here."

"No, Elvia," Marcial said. "Take the campesinos out now. If we don't get what we want during the negotiations, we'll come right back again."

"OK," I said, "we'll leave the offices, but we won't go home. We'll stay right across the street in the park until you're finished."

So Marcial went to negotiate with the military, while the rest of us waited in the park. Some of the campesinos went to sleep on the benches, others on the ground.

We waited and waited. At 1 a.m. they finally returned. "OK," we said, "what's the agreement? Because if we don't like it, we'll keep on fighting."

Marcial told us to calm down and said we could all go home because we got what we wanted. The next day all 105 of the campesinos were freed, and the ten groups got the land they were fighting for. It just goes to show that here in Honduras we don't get anything unless we fight for it.

It gives us a lot of courage to know we're not alone in our struggle. There are a lot of professional people, university professors, lawyers, doctors who help us. Lawyers who defend us and don't charge us a penny. Doctors who treat us for free. Professors who get on the radio to denounce the authorities when we get captured.

And when we're doing a land recovery, the campesino groups that have already won their own land help out. Sometimes they join in the recovery, sometimes they send food or money. They always help out in some way.

There are also workers' unions that help us. For example, the last time I was in jail the workers at INA in Comayagua put up money for my bail.

Our ties with the workers are very important. We in the CNTC realize that if we want to have any strength, we have to support the workers and vice versa. That's why we're part of the workers' federation called the FUTH, the United Federation of Honduran Workers. When other FUTH unions go on strike, we give them whatever help we can. And when we have land recoveries or are in trouble, they do what they can for us.

A few years ago there was a strike of hospital workers in Comayagua, which is the biggest town in our region. The nurses and hospital staff in Comayagua often help us when we have problems. I've gone to them at times and said, "Look, in such-and-such a place the campesinos are going hungry and their children are sick. Their stomachs are bloated from worms and they need medicines." And the workers have given us vitamins, iron, or medicines for the children. And when we have a land recovery or some other action, they often get on the radio and send a message of support.

So when the staff in Comayagua decided to go on strike, they called the campesino leaders together—there were seven of us—and asked for our support. They explained that they wanted to replace the head of the hospital because of the way he treated the workers—the nurses, the assistants, the janitors. And they were asking for a raise because they said their salaries weren't enough to live on. We thought their demands were just and decided to help them.

When they went on strike, they took over the whole hospital. The military surrounded the hospital, but the strikers kept the doors closed and wouldn't let them in. The situation was tense. The military said all the strikers would be jailed. They threatened to get them out with tear gas. But they knew that if they filled the hospital with tear gas, the patients inside would suffer.

So we went to get help from the campesino groups we work with. We told them there was a strike in the hospital and that the workers had asked for our support. When the campesinos agreed to help, the union sent a truck to bring them in—250 campesinos, both men and women.

We couldn't use the main entrance because it was surrounded by military, so we went in through the back—through the morgue. When the news came over the radio that hundreds of campesinos were in the hospital supporting the workers, other campesinos came in from the hills and took over the streets.

The military saw this great mass of people and didn't know what to do. Over the loudspeakers they told the campesinos to go home. They said the strike was a problem between the management of the hospital and the workers, that it had nothing to do with the campesinos.

I was in the hospital helping to organize the campesinos when a group of nurses ran up to me. "Elvia, Elvia," they said, "we heard soldiers talking to some of the campesina women. The soldiers told them to leave. But the women said they wouldn't leave until you told them to, that you were the leader. So now they're looking for you."

I wasn't even scared. I think all the excitement gave me more courage, because I really didn't feel afraid. But I didn't want them to arrest me either.

"OK," I said, "Quick, give me a uniform to wear." The nurses dressed me up like one of the operating nurses and put me in the operating room, because they figured the military wouldn't go in there.

I put on one of those long green uniforms the operating nurses wear, a cap to cover my head, a mask over my face, and plastic gloves. I was almost completely covered. Just my eyes showed.

I went into the operating room and started arranging the equipment they have in there, like I was really going to operate. I got out those little instruments, the needles, the gauze. Another nurse was in there with me, plugging in these machines they use, looking very busy.

Two of the intelligence officers burst into the room. "Excuse us, señoritas," they said, "but have you seen Elvia Alvarado around?" I looked very annoyed and said, "Who the hell is Elvia Alvarado? What are you talking about? Can't you see we're about to operate in here?"

"We're looking for this campesina, Elvia," they said, "a rebellious woman who's always sticking her nose in places it doesn't belong. She's the one that told the campesinos to support this strike."

"Look," I said, getting very mad, "I don't know who this woman is, and I've got more important things to do than worry about some stupid campesina. And on your way out," I said, "please close the door because these instruments are very delicate and we must keep them at just the right temperature."

When they left, we laughed and laughed. "Boy are they stupid," the other nurse said. "They didn't even recognize your voice." And we laughed and laughed.

We left the operating room and found that the situation was getting worse. The soldiers were threatening to throw tear gas into the hospital and to arrest all the campesinos. The campesinos were afraid that they would suffocate.

I got together three of the best campesinos and told them to control the group. I explained that if the soldiers threw tear gas, they should tell the people to get down on the ground. We got out boxes of sheets and I told them that if they threw tear gas, everyone should grab a sheet, soak it in water, and cover their faces with it. They should cover their heads with the wet sheet and get down on the ground, because the gas moves up. They should stay like that until the smoke clears.

I told them that if someone was tired and wanted to sleep, they could go to sleep on the floor, under the tables or benches. And most importantly, I told them to keep everyone calm.

An emergency commission had just arrived from the capital, and the union leaders, the director, and the commission had started to negotiate. We knew we just had to hold out a while longer.

By 4 a.m., the union came to an agreement with the management. They felt it was a good compromise, that they got most of what they were asking for. The fight was over, and the union sent for the truck to take the campesinos home. The nurses were afraid the police were still on the lookout for me, so they gave me a white uniform to wear and I went out the front door as if I were a nurse.

I went home exhausted but proud that we had helped the strikers put up a good fight. Because our job as campesino organizers is not just to work for a better life for the campesinos, it's to help all people who are fighting to make a decent living.

It's not easy to be an organizer. It's hard to keep any kind of family life, because we're always on the move. I leave my house for two weeks at a time, sometimes 20 days, sometimes a month. I spend most of my time with the campesinos in their communities. But I also visit the union offices in the capital, the INA offices in Comayagua, and the agencies that give us money for projects.

The communities we work in are hard to get to. I have to walk miles and miles, with my pack on my back, along the dirt trails. I get there exhausted from walking all day. Sometimes the sun is so hot I get drenched in sweat. Sometimes I get soaked by the rain. Sometimes I don't eat all day, and in the summertime the streams dry up and there's often no water to drink.

The campesinos are generous—they want to offer you something to eat, something to drink. But sometimes they can't. They barely have enough to keep themselves going. So the organizer suffers, because we work with the poorest.

It's affecting my health, because I'm not young any more. I'm 48 years old and starting to feel the years. I get tired, and I also have stomach problems from eating so irregularly. My stomach always hurts; I think the doctor said it's an ulcer.

I wish I could take better care of my daughters, because they have nothing. Lidia and her baby are completely dependent on me; she doesn't have a man to support her. And my other daughters are married to poor men.

They worry about me all the time, too. Sometimes they say to me, "No, mama. Don't do this work any more. They're going to kill you and we're the ones who are going to suffer. We don't want to lose you."

But I tell them, "It's because I love you so much that I must keep working. Because one day you're the ones who will benefit from this struggle—if not you then your children and your grandchildren. So don't tell me to leave my work. I know what I'm doing, and I know why I'm doing it. I'm doing it for you."

Sometimes when I'm in the city I see signs, "Help wanted. $150 a month." And I think how nice it would be to have a steady income. I think how much easier it would be on me and my family.

Because the CNTC can't afford to pay us regular salaries. We don't even call it a salary, we call it "financial aid." When there's money, I get $100 a month. When there's not money, I get $50, $25—whatever we can afford.

I really don't make enough money to live on, and that's why I'm in big trouble right now. Last year I had a lot of financial problems—my grandchild was sick, I got sick, and then I needed money to fix the house. So I borrowed money from a neighbor. She's a widow and although she's poor, her husband left her some money when he died. I know she needs the money because she has children to bring up. And I know I have to pay it back, because she was good enough to lend it to me—without any interest either. But I borrowed and borrowed and borrowed, and before I knew it I owed her $350. And now she wants to take my house away from me.

I got into debt because it was a time when the CNTC didn't have any money. We were in a great financial crisis. No one was getting paid, and a lot of the money I borrowed was to keep the work going. I had to keep visiting the groups. I had to travel. And every time you step out of the house, you start spending money. Every time you get on a bus, you have to pay. So I got deep into debt, just like most of the other organizers during that time.

I went to the CNTC and told them my problem. Because the CNTC is like my family. Whatever problems I have, even if they're personal problems, I take them to my compañeros. Say one of my children or grandchildren died, or one of my children was taken to jail, or I got sick. Whatever it is, I call the CNTC for help.

So I told the CNTC about my debt, and they said they'd try to help me pay the money back. Not all of it, but a part of it. Because they don't want me to be out in the street again. My little house is the only thing I have. It's taken me so many years to get it. If I lose it, where am I going to find a place to live—with all my children and grandchildren?

Despite all our financial problems, we know that we have to keep working, whether or not we have money. We're not doing this work to get rich; we're not government employees who just go to collect our weekly paychecks. And we're not a factory either, so we can't fight for higher wages. We're a poor campesino organization, and we have to make do with the little we have. Money or no money, we have to keep up the struggle.

Sometimes when I don't have money, my daughters make tortillas in the house and go out and sell them. Or they cook beans to sell. Or they make candies. Sometimes they give me a dollar or two so I can keep working. And when I get to a campesino group, one family gives me food. Another lends me a horse to get to the next group. Another gives me bus fare so I can return home. That's my life. That's my work.

But I know I'd never trade my work for a job with a steady salary. Never. I've had the chance. The government has tried to buy me out. They offered me a job in the capital for $300 a month. Imagine me with a salary of $300 a month! I could live like a king.

But all they really wanted was to get me out of the countryside and tucked away safely at some desk in the city, buried in a pile of papers. I've seen it happen to other campesino leaders before. Once they get a government job they start riding around in fancy cars, their wallets are full, and they forget all about the rest of the campesinos.

But I couldn't be happy if my belly was full while my neighbors didn't have a plate of beans and tortillas to put on the table. My struggle is for a better life for all Hondurans, and my principles are worth more than $300 a month.

Someone can come and offer me $500, or $1,000, or $2,000. My principles are not for sale. The struggle is my life. When I'm hungry, when I'm thirsty, when I don't have a cent, the struggle keeps me going.

"We're not going to solve our problems
through handouts. Until we change the system
all the charity in the world won't take us out
of poverty."

10

We Don't Want to Beg

Honduras is full of foreign organizations that say they're here to help our country. I know a lot of these foreign groups—AID (the U.S. Agency for International Development), the United Nations, the Food and Agriculture Organization, the Peace Corps. Honduras is swamped by foreigners, most of them from the United States. But that's not the solution for our problems.

Honduras is a rich country. In my work I get to travel all over the country, and I've seen just how rich it is. We've got everything here—good land, water, minerals, forests. If we used what we had in the right way, we could take care of ourselves without going to the United States or other countries for help.

The land here is rich, but it doesn't belong to us. Large parts of it are controlled by the banana companies, and all their profits are taken out of the country. The same with our forests. The government just sold off a whole chunk of our forests to a gringo, even though the law says you can't sell state land to foreigners. They just put some Honduran's name on the paper, but everyone knows the real owner is the gringo.

The same with our minerals. Honduras has lots of minerals—gold, copper, silver. We have these big mining companies, like the Rosario Mining Company. They take all these minerals and ship them out of the country, and they don't leave anything for us Hondurans.

Honduras isn't poor, but our riches leave the country. Most of it goes to the United States. And then we have to go back to the gringos and beg to get some of it back. What a racket! They get rich off our wealth, and then we get down on our hands and knees begging for help.

It seems to me that the United States wants us to be begging for money all the time; it doesn't want us to be independent. We thought the last president Suazo Córdova was bad, but this president—Azcona—has been even worse. In the last few years, Honduras has become more and more dependent on the United States.

But the millions of dollars the gringos send don't help the poor campesinos. The money isn't used to create jobs so that everyone can work. Instead the money is for arms, for airplanes, for war tanks. But we don't eat airplanes, we don't eat tanks, we don't eat bullets. The only things we campesinos eat is corn and beans. So what good are all those weapons?

A lot of the money the U.S. sends is used to build roads. But they're mainly interested in building roads that lead to military bases or the Nicaraguan border. They're opening up lots of new roads in the south—in Choluteca and El Paraíso and the Mosquitia—because that's where the contras are fighting the Sandinistas.

Why don't they build roads in other parts of the country, like in the villages where the poor campesinos live? When you want to get to a campesino village, you might have to walk three or four hours straight uphill on dirt trails. If a road isn't important for the government or the gringos, forget it. It never gets paved.

Another thing the United States sends to help us is the Peace Corps. The Peace Corps has been in Honduras for a long time, but now there are more of these volunteers than ever. They say it's the biggest Peace Corps program in the world. But to tell you the truth, I really don't understand what they're doing. I see them working in some of the communities I visit, but a lot of their work doesn't make any sense to me.

The only direct contact I had was with a Peace Corps volunteer I met through some friends. She said she was helping women set up gardens so they would have more food for their families. It sounded good to me, so I invited her to meet with one of the women's groups I work with. Well, she came and met with them and got all the women very enthused. But then she never came back again. I later heard that she'd been sent back to the states. And I think that's one of the main problems with these Peace Corps people—they're here today and gone tomorrow. So the programs they set up often fall apart when they leave.

Another complaint I've heard about the Peace Corps people is that they insist on working with individuals instead of groups. They say the groups have too many problems. But aren't they supposed to be working where the problems are?

If they really want to have the most impact, they'd be working with the organized groups of campesinos. But there are Peace Corps volunteers who live in communities where the people are organized, and the volunteers don't even know the organizations exist. They don't bother to work with the structures we're struggling so hard to set up.

Of course, there are those who say that the Peace Corps is just a front for the CIA. Who knows? I suppose there must be some CIA people in there. And I'm sure there are also many good, sincere people as well. All I know is that they're certainly no solution to our poverty, and they're not bringing us any closer to peace.

The Peace Corps can send more and more people, the United Nations can have more and more projects, AID can be here for a century—and our problems would still exist. Because all these institutions are invited by the government; they all work through the government. So for us they're just part of the system that keeps us poor.

There are a few groups that don't work through the government. There's this group Pueblo to People that works directly with the campesinos. They buy things from the cooperatives—things like handicrafts and cashew nuts—and sell them in the United States. But groups like Pueblo to People are few and their budgets are small. And the government can always kick out a group it doesn't like.

In my village there's a project called New Dawn. They have a cafeteria where they feed the children a hot meal every day. There are so many children who want to join that they can't take them all. There are now 500 children in the program and more on the waiting list. Every child has gringo godparents in the United States. The gringos send the child a picture of their family, write letters, and send gifts once in a while.

My granddaughter is in the program. Her godparents sent us a picture of their family on Christmas. They have two children, with blond hair and big round faces. They live in a town called Iowa.

The program is a good one because the children get food every day, and they need the food. It's the only good meal my granddaughter gets.

I'm very grateful to all these organizations in the United States, especially the private and religious organizations. I appreciate the food and clothing they send. I thank them sincerely for their willingness to help, and I know they do it with great love.

But I'd also like to say that this relationship—where we're dependent on the goodwill of outsiders—isn't the kind of relationship we'd like to have. It's not our ideal kind of exchange.

Because this way we're always waiting for handouts. We're always waiting for foreign institutions to come and give us food, to give us clothing, to give us dollars. In the long run, we're no better off.

We're not going to solve our problem through handouts. Because our problem is a social one. And until we change this system, all the charity in the world won't take us out of poverty.

How can we ever get out of poverty if we can't get a piece of land to work? If we had land to plant, we wouldn't need to get food sent to us all the way from the United States. No. We'd have our own. But as long as the government refuses to give us the land and other resources we need, we'll continue to beg from the United States, and we'll continue to have foreigners running our country.

We Hondurans are capable of doing anything, if we had the education. But instead of teaching Hondurans, the government brings in these foreign experts with their huge salaries. And we continue to be idiots. We don't know how to administer our wealth, so people from other countries have to come to do it for us.

I've heard people say that the workers don't have the ability to run a factory. But that's because the owners hide the information they need to run it. So maybe they can't right now, but why couldn't they in the future?

And what about us campesinos? Don't we have the ability to run the big farms? As it is now, the landowners just drop by their ranches on the weekend to have a good time. It's the campesinos who do all the work. So why shouldn't we be the owners?

Las Isletas is a good example of what the workers can do. When Hurricane Fifi destroyed a lot of the banana lands belonging to the Standard Fruit Company, the Company was just going to leave the land idle. So the workers took it over. They fixed it all up and did such a good job that they grew more bananas on the land than Standard ever did. But Standard didn't like the competition, so it paid some of the local military men to arrest the leaders and put some lackeys in their place.

That was the end of the experiment, but it proved that the workers can run a big business. It proved how much sense it makes for the workers to own the factories and the campesinos to own the farms.

And why shouldn't we? We're human beings. We have the same five senses God gave everyone. We have eyes, ears, feet, and hands—just like these big pricks that come here bossing us around.

A little while ago I took a course in administration that the CNTC gave us. It's important for us to learn about administration, so that one day when we get a chance to run the country we'll know how to do it.

It's not so difficult to be an administrator, you know. I think we campesinos would be better at running the economy than the ones running the country now. Especially us women.

When you come to think of it, campesina women are terrific administrators. With the measly dollar a day the men give us, we buy corn, beans, sugar, salt, rice, oil, and coffee. If we can run our homes on a dollar a day, we'd surely do a better job running our country than these rich guys can.

What do they know about being thrifty? What do they know about "making do"? What do they know about sharing? Nothing. Wait till you see what a good job we do when we get a chance to run the country!

We'll spread the wealth. We'll distribute the land, we'll get the banana companies in line, we'll take good care of our minerals and forests. And we won't depend on the United States or anyone else. We women like our independence.

Hondurans don't want to be beggars. We're tired of begging from the United States. We want to be equals. And to be equals we need more than charity; we need solidarity.

I'd say the best way to show solidarity with us is not by sending food or clothing or dollars. No. Show your solidarity by telling your government that Honduras belongs to the Hondurans. Tell your government to get out of our country and leave us alone. And stand by us in our struggle.

"I used to feel hatred towards the gringo soldiers. But now I know these poor gringos are just ignorant; they don't know why they're here or what this struggle is all about."

American soldiers on maneuvers in Honduras.

11

Gringos and Contras
on Our Land

Ever since the Sandinistas came to power, the United States has been building bases all over our country. I live next to Palmerola, the biggest U.S. base. I don't know how far I live from Palmerola, because I really don't know how to measure it. By bus it takes 20 minutes. And if you walk through the fields, it's even closer. At night we can see the lights of the base from our house, and during the day we see the planes and helicopters flying overhead. They pass right over our houses.

I've never been to Palmerola, so I don't know what's really going on there. But I don't understand why these gringo bases are here to begin with.

First of all, they kicked a lot of campesino groups off their lands to make room for the bases. Take the Palmerola base—there were two campesino groups there before, and they moved them to another piece of land that isn't as good.

Secondly, the bases only strengthen the Honduran military, and that means more repression for us.

I used to feel hatred towards the gringo soldiers. Why should they be in our country, with all their guns and all their dollars, making life even more difficult for us? But now I know that these poor gringos are just ignorant; they really don't know why they're here or what this struggle is all about. I have friends who've talked to some of them, and they say that these guys don't know anything about Central

America. They've just been sent here by their government. So it's really not their fault; it's the fault of the people who sent them here.

Sure, there are some people who are delighted to have the gringos here. They say, "Isn't it great we have these gringos here protecting our country?" Others are happy because the gringos spend their money here. In Comayagua, which is the town nearest the Palmerola base, the businessmen are happy to have their dollars. The people who own restaurants and bars are happy. And of course the prostitutes are happy.

There was a big scandal when the gringos first came, because the level of prostitution shot up something terrible. I won't say there weren't any prostitutes before, but not like this—with whole streets full of bordellos. The Honduran men got pissed because the prostitutes were only interested in dollars, they didn't want to sleep with Hondurans any more. And of course their prices went up, too.

There was also a scandal around the sexual abuse of children by the gringos. There were cases of children who were raped. We'd never had anything like that before the gringos came here.

And people started talking about a sexual disease called the "flor de Vietnam," the flower of Vietnam. I guess it's named after that country Vietnam, where the United States fought another war. All I know is that it's a sexual disease that's hard to cure.

But the worst thing has been AIDS. There've been six cases of AIDS in Comayagua, and the people are sure it came from the gringos.

There was a terrible panic here when they discovered the first cases of AIDS. People said that if you caught AIDS you'd only live for 40 days. They said that when gringos got AIDS they lasted longer, because they had better defenses than we Indians have. There was even a hit song on the radio that said, "The girls should watch out for AIDS, the old women should watch out for AIDS, the queers should watch out for AIDS, everyone watch out for AIDS."

People said you could get AIDS from a kiss, from making love, from queers, from needles, from saliva. So there were a lot of people who wouldn't go into restaurants any more, because they were afraid of drinking out of someone else's glass. When I'd go into a public bathroom, I wouldn't sit on the toilet any more, but way up in the air so I wouldn't get AIDS.

One day I was visiting one of the women's groups near the river. I suggested that we go fishing to try to catch something for lunch. But they said, "No, Elvia. On the radio we heard that even the fish have AIDS because the women's bodies were thrown here."

There was a rumor that two prostitutes in Santa Barbara died of AIDS and that the government threw their bodies in the Yojoa River. Others said that when the women found out they had AIDS they panicked and threw themselves into the river. But everyone in the area said that the river was poisoned with AIDS and couldn't be touched.

"Don't be ridiculous," I said. "Even if the bodies were thrown in the river, they'd be long gone by now. The current would've taken them and the AIDS with them. Let's go in." And we did.

The next day, I started feeling bumps on my ass, and other bumps on my ankles. I said to myself, "Oh my God, now I have AIDS! Why the hell did I go in that water?" I panicked. But soon the bumps went away by themselves.

Another big problem for Honduras is the presence of the contras. The government can deny it all it wants, but everyone knows the contras are all over our country.

The contras make life hard for Hondurans living on the border. Coffee growers in the south lost their entire crop because of the fighting. These are poor farmers, not big plantation owners. I heard on the radio that they all marched to the capital to complain to the president and ask him to kick the contras out. Then they went to the U.S. embassy and asked them to pay for their losses, but the gringos said it wasn't their problem.

Where I live you don't see contras, because it's not close to the Nicaraguan border. I say you don't see them, but they might very well be there, because the Honduran military is so corrupt that it's selling its own uniforms to the contras. So you really don't know who's who any more, since there are contras going around as Hondurans. Can you imagine that? How can the military stoop so low as to sell its own uniforms? Doesn't it have any sense of dignity? Everything in our country is for sale now—from women's bodies to the army's uniforms!

Anyway, one time I was at a meeting in the south. It was right near the border between Honduras and Nicaragua where the contras have their bases. After the meeting I went around talking to the people there. I always want to learn everything I can. I'm always asking questions.

So I talked with people who lived near the border and they told me they were afraid because there was fighting going on there all the time, right near their homes. They said that the contras live on the Honduran side of the border, and they sneak into Nicaragua when the Sandinistas aren't looking. They throw bombs and plant mines—and when the Sandinistas go after them, they run back into Honduras.

The people who live near the border are scared to death, because they get caught in the battles. Lots of campesinos have moved. They say there are now thousands of Hondurans who are homeless because of the contra war.

Everyone knows that if it weren't for the contras, there'd be no problems with the Sandinistas. Nobody thinks the Sandinistas are interested in taking over Honduras. They've already got one poor country to worry about. Why would they want another one?

But the campesinos down there are scared of the contras. They're scared about getting deeper into a war with Nicaragua, and they're scared to talk about their fears. They talk to me because I'm one of them. But they won't talk to outsiders, because there are lots of Honduran soldiers in the area. They say the soldiers told them not to talk to anyone, especially journalists.

Our government allows these contras to hide out here, but who are the ones to suffer? The Hondurans. Which Hondurans? The poor. The soldiers in the army, you see, are not the sons of the rich. Never. The sons of the rich are untouchable. They go to fancy schools or they hang around the street smoking marijuana. But the sons of the poor go into the army.

They recruit the campesinos by force. I know cases where the army has gone to the campesino settlements and taken away young boys right from the fields. They make the sons of the poor fight against their own brothers and sisters, against their own people or against their brothers and sisters in Nicaragua.

Just a few days ago we heard the news that a Honduran military plane crashed near the Nicaraguan border. It was a plane that the United States sold to Honduras. I don't know what kind it was—I don't understand all that stuff about DCs and F2s. All I know is that it was a plane carrying 52 people—colonels, lieutenants, sergeants, soldiers, and a few civilians, including children. All 52 of them died; there wasn't a survivor in the lot.

No one knows exactly what happened—if the Nicaraguans shot it down, if there was something wrong with the plane, or what.

Fifty-two Hondurans died, and the whole country was in mourning. But no one asked why they died. They asked what happened to the plane, but they didn't ask why the plane was there to begin with.

The base they were flying to was a base in the Mosquitia. Before the gringos were around, Honduras never had an air base in the Mosquitia. Why should we? The Mosquitia's in the middle of nowhere—just a lot of mountains and trees. We're not such a rich country that we can afford to have bases in the middle of nowhere. No. It was the U.S. that built that airstrip. If we hadn't been dragged into this U.S. war, those 52 Hondurans wouldn't have been there to begin with.

But all the government says is, "Oh, what a terrible tragedy. Oh, the poor Colonel and the poor lieutenants and the poor little boy and their poor families. Oh, the Honduran people are in mourning." But they don't say anything about why they died, about why the Honduran military is flying around the Nicaraguan border.

Instead of all the condolences and the mourning, why doesn't the government say, "That's enough. We've had it with the U.S. bases and the U.S. military and this U.S. war. We won't be cannon fodder for the United States. Enough!"

Campesinos don't want war. War only makes our lives more difficult than they already are. What we want is land and jobs, not war. War only means a lot of poor people will die. We've got enough problems without fighting the rich man's war.

I'd like to know how the United States thinks this whole thing is going to end. What's going to happen to the contras? How long are they going to stay in Honduras? Forever?

Because I don't think they'll ever win, unless they have U.S. troops fighting with them. So what's going to happen to them? They can't go back to Nicaragua, because they've killed too many people. They've caused too much suffering for the Nicaraguans to let them back in. So will they stay here in Honduras? That's what worries us.

I don't understand what the United States plans to do. I don't think they'd send in U.S. troops, because the Sandinistas are well prepared and too many gringos would die. I don't think they'd bomb Nicaragua, either. Because if they bombed Nicaragua, that other nation—the Soviet Union— would get involved, and the United States is afraid of a war with the Soviet Union. It doesn't mind a war with little countries like Nicaragua, but it doesn't want a war with the Soviet Union. Then all hell would break loose. So just where is the United States going with all this? Why doesn't it just leave Nicaragua alone?

I don't understand why Ronald Reagan hates Nicaragua so much. What has Nicaragua done to Ronald? I don't know where he got this hatred from.

Maybe Nicaragua did something to the United States that I don't know about. But it seems that the United States just wants to dominate all of Central America. And since Nicaragua doesn't want to be dominated, that's why the United States hates it. Because Nicaragua refuses to give in.

I've been thinking about this a lot. It seems to me that if Ronald Reagan loses in Nicaragua, he'll lose in all of Central America. But if he defeats Nicaragua, then he's got it made. He's already got Honduras, so that's two countries. And with Nicaragua and Honduras he can go on to take El Salvador. That's three Central American republics under U.S. control. Then Guatemala will follow. That's what Ronald Reagan wants. And he knows that if he loses in Nicaragua, he loses all his interests in Central America.

If I could talk to Ronald Reagan, I'd tell him he's on the wrong track. I'd tell him to stop being so unjust with us Central Americans.

Sometimes I think that I shouldn't be talking like this, because maybe Ronald will tell the Hondurans to get rid of me. And since the Honduran government does everything the United States says, I'd be a dead duck.

But to tell you the truth, I think that Ronald's government is the stupidest government I've seen in my life. He calls us communists, but he's the one that's doing all the damage. If it's true that communists are so bad, that they take away all your freedom, then our government in Honduras is communist, and Ronald Reagan is the biggest communist of them all!

I don't understand what business Ronald has sticking his nose into Nicaragua. And what business does he have in Honduras? Someone needs to have a heart-to-heart talk with Ronald and tell him that things in Central America have to change, whether he likes it or not.

"Here all the money goes for the military. And we poor Hondurans? Malnourished, without land to work, without jobs, without education. Is that a democracy?"

12

What's Democracy?
What's Communism?

They say we have a democracy in Honduras, because when there's not a coup we have elections every four years. But democracy means more than just elections. Democracy means that all people have the same rights. Democracy means that we all have the same opportunities, that we all have the right to live a decent life. Maybe there's democracy for the rich, but certainly not for the poor.

Let me give you the example of what happened to my friend Carmen. Carmen was married to Juan, and they had six children. When the children were still quite young, Juan got cancer and died. Poor Carmen was left to fend for herself. She had a small piece of land that she and the children used to grow food to feed themselves. It wasn't much, but at least they weren't starving.

Héctor González, a big politician with the Liberal Party, had some property next to her house. There was only a small road leading to his property, and he wanted to build a bigger road so his car could get through. But the land leading to his property belonged to Carmen. When Juan was alive, Héctor had tried to buy it from him, but Juan refused because they needed the land.

Soon after Juan's death, Héctor decided to go after the land again. He went to INA and claimed he was the legal owner. Carmen is a poor, shy woman. She wouldn't scare a mouse. So when this big Héctor came around saying the land was his, she didn't know what to do. And of course the director of INA was on Héctor's side, since Héctor was a big shot in the Liberal Party and the Liberals were in power.

Carmen was a nervous wreck. Héctor was trying to take away her land, and she was afraid her son would try to kill him. Because her son Jorge was mad. "Listen," he said to his mother, "that bastard's not gonna get our land. I'll fix him with this .22. That'll teach him to respect our property."

Carmen came looking for me. "Elvia, Elvia," she said, in tears, "I need your help. Héctor González wants to take away my land. I'm a poor widow. You know I need that land for my children. It's the only thing my husband left me. How can he do this to me? And to make matters worse, my son Jorge is ready to kill him."

The next day I went to INA with her. We took her land title and went to see the director. The director said Carmen had to give up the land so Héctor would have access to his property.

"Carmen's my friend," I said, "and I've come to defend her. She's a poor widow with six children and she needs every inch of land she can get. And Héctor has no right to the land because it's planted with corn and beans, so according to the law it's fulfilling its social function. Besides, that rich bastard's got plenty of land, more than he needs. He shouldn't go stealing land from a poor widow."

The director told us he couldn't decide the case, that we'd have to take it to court. Well, of course Héctor could afford a good lawyer and Carmen couldn't. So who do you think won the case?

In a democracy we're all supposed to be equal before the law, but in Honduras the rich are more equal than the poor. In a democracy if you break the law you're supposed to get punished, right? But here in Honduras the rich don't get punished, only the poor. The rich don't go to jail when they kill campesinos or labor leaders. The rich don't go to jail when they violate the Agrarian Reform Law. The rich don't go to jail when they steal from the people. No, the law only applies to the poor.

Look at what happened with CONADI, a government corporation that lends money to big businessmen. The heads of CONADI took money from the government and stuffed it in their own bank accounts or loaned it to their friends, who never paid the money back. So now we're told that CONADI is missing $300 million and has gone bankrupt! Can you imagine that? They steal $300 million from the people and get away scot-free.

What about these corrupt politicians? Look at Osvaldo López. When he was president he took a million-dollar bribe from the banana companies. What about this deputy Rodolfo Zelaya, who got rich off the money the United States was sending to the contras? Do the corrupt politicians ever go to jail? The worst that happens to them is that they leave the country and live like kings somewhere else, enjoying all the money they stole.

No, it's the campesino who goes to jail for stealing a chicken or a cow or a few ears of corn. A campesino can spend years in jail for stealing a chicken, but the thieves who steal millions never go to jail. Because they're the ones in power. They're not about to put themselves in jail.

So when I fight with the police and the military and they say to me, "You've got to respect the law," I just laugh. I say, "Look, don't talk to me about laws. When you start respecting the law, we'll start respecting it. You have to set the example, but the laws mean nothing to you. You all wipe your ass with the laws. So how can you tell us to respect them?"

Another thing about a democratic country is that you're supposed to have the right to say what you want. Isn't that part of a democracy? But here in Honduras there's no freedom of speech. Look what happens to people who protest against the government, or against the contra camps and the gringo bases in our country. The only day we get to say things openly is on May 1st, which is International Workers' Day. All the popular organizations march through the streets and shout whatever we feel like shouting.

But even then we're in trouble. Look what happened to the union leader Cristóbal Pérez. He was a great leader, because his goal was to try to unite the different worker and campesino groups. On May 1, 1986, he led a big march in which all the different groups participated. And at the rally he spoke out against U.S. and contra troops in Honduras. Well, a week later, he was shot dead in front of his house. So that's why people are afraid to say what they think.

The journalists used to have more freedom than anyone, but now look what's happening to them. The armed forces said that anyone who speaks out against the contras in

Honduras is a subversive. They put a bomb in the car of Wong Arevalo, a journalist on the radio. They tried to blow him up because of his commentaries, because he said something critical about the military and the contras.

I used to think that some of the big shots could get away with criticizing the government—people like Guatama Fonseca, who used to be Minister of Labor; or Juan Almendares, who was president of the university; or Efraín Díaz Arrivillaga, who's a delegate for the Christian Democrats; or Víctor Meza, who heads this research center. But now the papers published a death list that someone found, and who do you think's on the list? Guatama Fonseca, Juan Almendares, Efraín Díaz, Víctor Meza, and about ten others like them.

Ramón Custodio, the head of the Honduran Human Rights Commission, was also on the list. And since then, he's had bombs thrown at his home—just because he speaks out against human rights abuses. So what freedom is left here?

Another thing a democratic government has to do is take care of the people. It has to spend money on things that make people's lives better. Here the government spends more money on the military than it does on health and education. Last year, while millions of Hondurans are sick and illiterate, they cut the budgets for education and health. Why? So there'd be more money to buy more weapons, more airplanes, more tanks.

Here all the money goes for the military. All the money goes for the rich. And we poor Hondurans? Malnourished, without land to work, without jobs, without education. Is that a democracy?

So the only thing we have in Honduras is the right to vote—when there's not a coup, that is. But who can we vote for? The two main parties, the Liberals and the Nationalists (or the *cachurecos*, as we call them, the conservatives) are the same crap. They're full of corrupt politicians who just want to get rich quick. There's no difference between the two parties, they just trade off every few years to make it look democratic.

Everybody in Honduras votes. Here the people love to vote, they stand in long lines to vote. Election day is a big holiday. But why? Because the people are so excited about the candidates? No. Because on election day the politicians kill a bunch of cows and give away lots of food, lots of meat. For many people it's one of their only chances to eat meat.

In this last election there were four parties running—the Liberals and the Nationalists, and then two smaller parties, the Christian Democrats and the PINU (Innovation and Unity Party). They all set up their booths with food, but the Liberals and the Nationalists are the richest so they have the best spread.

You're only supposed to take food from the party you vote for. But the campesinos are no dummies. The vote is secret; no one knows who they voted for. So they go to the Liberal Party's booth and say, "Long live the Liberals," and they get their food. Then they go to the Nationalists and say, "Long live the Nationalists," and they get some more food. And then they get the rest from the two other parties. So election day is a great feast for the campesinos. But little do they know how much that bit of meat really costs them.

When I talk to the campesinos, they blame the government for not looking out for them. They blame the traditional parties—the National and Liberal parties. But then they turn around and vote for these parties. You ask poor Hondurans why they vote for the Nationalist Party and they'll say, "Oh, because my grandfather and my great grandfather were Nationalists. I was born a Nationalist." The same with the Liberals—their mothers, their fathers, their grandfathers were Liberals, so they are too.

So we're really the ones to blame, because we vote for these parties. We're the majority in this country. We're the ones that put these corrupt politicians in power. Because most of the poor are still ignorant and continue to vote for the traditional parties.

I don't vote for them, I vote for the Christian Democrats. But I don't tell the campesinos to vote Christian Democrat. We at the union are still working out our position on voting—whether we should vote for one of the new parties, or not vote at all, or form our own party.

In the meantime we try to make the campesinos aware that the traditional parties are no solution. We know this process of education is a long one, but that's why we're organizing people and teaching them their rights.

If everyone realized that we have the right to participate in our government, we'd have a different government. We wouldn't be electing the people we're electing today. The government would be for the majority. People would respect the law. And then we could say that Honduras is really a democratic country.

I don't know how democratic Nicaragua is. The radio says everything is terrible in Nicaragua and that the government is repressive—that they force the young boys to fight the war, and if they refuse they kill them. They say that the people are starving, that there's no food, nothing in the stores. They say that everyone wants to leave, that even the Sandinistas are trying to escape.

On the radio you always hear from the Nicaraguans who've left. "Why did you leave Nicaragua?" the journalists ask them. "I left Nicaragua because in Nicaragua there's no food," they say. Or they say, "I left because the government is repressive. They're a bunch of dirty communists." But we never get a chance to hear from the Nicaraguans that didn't leave.

A while back the Honduran government was denouncing the closing of that newspaper *La Prensa* and asking Honduran journalists to denounce it. But we never heard the Sandinista side of the story, so how can we decide what the truth is?

I would love to go to Nicaragua and see for myself what's happening there. I would love to see how their president, this guy Daniel Ortega, is doing, and whether or not Nicaraguans are participating in their government. I wouldn't expect everyone to participate, because there will always be people who are against the changes and won't participate. But the majority. I'd like to see if they're really participating, and then make up my own mind about the Sandinistas.

But if a Honduran goes to Nicaragua, you're labeled communist. The authorities go around asking, "What was so-and-so doing in Nicaragua?" You couldn't continue your work, because they'd be after you all the time, saying you were a communist. I don't know anyone who's been to Nicaragua. They wouldn't take the risk.

We hear that the United States is a great democracy. I don't know much about what things are like inside the United States. I used to think there were only rich people in the United States. But now I learned that there are rich and poor there, just like in Honduras. Maybe the poor aren't as poor as we are, but the United States is such a rich country there shouldn't be any poor people there. If it were a really democratic country, there wouldn't be people without homes and jobs.

But the real reason I know the United States isn't a democratic country is by looking at all the injustices it's committing in our countries. It's funding these contra terrorists to kill people in Nicaragua. It's killing lots of poor people in El Salvador. It's arming the Honduran military. That's not the sign of a democratic government. If the United States was democratic, it wouldn't be doing these things.

I don't know enough about the Soviet Union to know if there's democracy in that country. I've never met anyone from there. I don't even know what color they are or what language they speak. The only ones I know are the gringos, because they're the ones who've got all their bases here.

The only thing I've heard about the Soviet Union is that it's supporting the Sandinistas. But I don't know if it gives support the same way the United States does. When the United States gives support, it wants something in return. For the United States it's like a business deal. They give you money and then they own you. But I don't know if the Soviet Union has done that to Nicaragua.

I've never met a Cuban, either. They say the Cubans are communists, that the Cuban people don't have any freedom, that the country is run by this dictator Fidel Castro. But I also hear that in Cuba people have food, clothing, education, and medicine. So I think if my family has food, clothing, education, and medicine, what else would I want?

But they say, "No, in Cuba you have to work so many hours a day, day and night, whether you like it or not. And the government looks over your shoulder to make sure you're working."

Well, I've never been to Cuba to see if that's true or not. But what do they think? That a government should take care of people whether they work or not? We campesinos aren't afraid of hard work. Our biggest problem here is that we can't find work. With our great democracy, we're dying of hunger because we don't have any jobs, because we don't have any way to make a living.

If it's true that there's work in Cuba, what more could you want? Because where there's work, there's food, health, education—everything. If those things exist in Cuba, how happy the Cubans must be. And if that's communism, then thank God for communism.

I really don't understand what communism is. When they say to me, "You're nothing but a filthy communist!" I tell them that I don't even know what it means. "But you must," I say, "because you're the one calling me a communist. And if you know what it is, then maybe you're the communist, not me."

If someone doesn't like what you're doing, they label you a communist. But we campesinos aren't afraid of the Soviet Union. I've never seen a Soviet person in my life. But I've seen lots of gringos, almost all of them soldiers. So that's who we're afraid of—the United States.

They try to scare us about the threat of communism so we won't do anything, so we'll be so terrified of communism that we won't do anything about the terror we face today. They want us to keep our eyes closed and our mouths shut.

It's a weapon, a strong weapon, that the rich use against us—making us fear communism more than we fear them. That's how they destroy any movement for change.

We campesinos don't care about communism or socialism. We don't understand what they mean. What we do understand is injustice. What we do understand is that we have to fight for the right to live like human beings. We don't care what you call it—capitalism, socialism, communism, any ism.

Ronald Reagan goes around saying that Nicaragua is communist and that communism is a threat to Central America. Why doesn't he say that he's a big capitalist, and that capitalism has made a great mess of Central America? Why doesn't he talk about what capitalism has done? We don't know what communism is, but we sure know what capitalism has done for us!

They say we campesinos are stupid, and that the Russian communists will come and manipulate us. Maybe we're uneducated, because it's true we haven't had much chance to get an education. But we're not stupid. We don't want anyone manipulating us—Russians or gringos. But I'll tell you, we don't see any Russians trying to manipulate us. The only foreigners trying to manipulate us are the gringos.

We want to talk like equals. If the U.S. government ever called us to have a dialogue with them, to talk as equals instead of ordering us around, then we'd be willing to hear them out. Just like we'd be willing to talk to the Russians. Why shouldn't we? If we want other governments to listen to us, then we must listen to them as well. We want to dialogue with everyone, but on equal terms.

Reagan can't tell me what to do. Ortega can't tell me what to do. My own mother can't even tell me what to do, because my thoughts are my own.

"Since I'm not willing to stop my organizing work, I'm sure someday I'll be captured again. Every time I leave my house, I'm not sure whether I'll come back again."

13

Facing Repression and Prison

In Honduras the repressive forces have us all under control.
We're all on the blacklist—our names, where we live, where
we work, everything.

And the repression is getting worse. Before, the military
would jail the leaders and then let them go. But today the
best leaders, the most outspoken, the ones with the most
guts, they get "disappeared." They're captured and never
found again.

I've been in jail six times in the past few years, but the last
time was the worst. They treated me like they never did
before.

It all began, as usual, with a land recovery. This time there
were four campesino groups I was working with—El Rosario, Piedras Azules, El Buen Pastor, and 3 de Octubre. One of
the groups had been waiting for five years for INA to process
their request! They were all tired of waiting, and the planting
season was coming up so there was a lot of pressure to finally
do something.

We decided that all four groups would recover their land at
the same time, to create more problems for INA and to have
a stronger negotiating position. In all there were 500 of us. I
went around from group to group, supervising the
recoveries.

While I was visiting one of the groups, we got word that the military had been to another group looking for me. They said that I was a subversive and was stirring up the campesinos.

The campesinos told them, "No, Elvia's not to blame. If you want something to blame, blame our hunger. Blame the fact that we don't have corn, that we don't have beans, that we don't have a piece of land to farm. If you want to blame someone, don't blame Elvia. Blame the head of INA for not carrying out the Agrarian Reform Law."

When the head of INA heard them talking like that, he ordered the military to arrest them all. They took most of the campesinos off to jail.

The campesinos warned me that I should hide, because there was a warrant out for my arrest.

So I went into hiding in the mountains. The military went from village to village looking for me. It was the rainy season, and a lot of the time I had to sleep out in the rain with no cover. There's a part of the mountains that's full of caves, and I went there to sleep. But I still got sick from sleeping out in the cold.

A group of campesinos followed me everywhere, trying to protect me. I didn't sleep in the campesinos' houses because I didn't want to create problems for them. I knew the military would come to their villages looking for me.

Meanwhile, I was concerned about the campesinos in jail. I sent a message to the CNTC headquarters in Tegucigalpa, telling them that the others were in jail and needed help.

I don't know if the message got there or what, but no one from the CNTC showed up. And the campesinos sent word that they needed my help. It was me that they trusted. It was me they'd been working with. And I knew their wives were worried sick and were desperate to get them out of jail.

So I realized I had to stop hiding and go to town to help out. I snuck into town and met with a lawyer. But as soon as I left the lawyer's house and started walking through the park, I was stopped by two men. They were riding in one of the landowner's cars. "Señora, stop," they shouted. "Stop." But I just kept walking, pretending I didn't hear.

Then they jumped out of the car, ran over to me and stuck a gun in my stomach. They kept jabbing me in the stomach with the gun. The people in the park were all staring.

"What are you doing to me?" I screamed. "What's going on? You can't do this to me!"

"We told you to stop," they said. "We're the authorities." But they were dressed like civilians. Then I knew they were from the DNI, the National Department of Investigations, because the DNI always goes in plainclothes.

"Let's see your identification," I said. They took out their badges. "OK," I said, "let's go." We got in the car and they took me to the DNI headquarters.

When I was in the car, I wasn't scared. But as I was entering the DNI I got frightened, because all of a sudden I remembered that I had a copy of a Nicaraguan newspaper in my backpack. A few weeks before, when I was in the capital, someone had given it to me to look at.

I hadn't even been home since then, so it was still in my backpack. I never had the time to look at it, so I'd just stuck it in my pack, and the stupid thing was still in there.

"Uh-oh," I said to myself, "now I'm in for it. They'll kill me for carrying that damn newspaper." I didn't even know what it said, but it was from Nicaragua and that was bad enough.

When they took me to jail they emptied my pack out and went through everything I had in there. They looked at every telephone number and asked me about each one. I had the number of the CNTC, of some of the lawyers we work with, of some of the groups that support us.

"Why do you have so many phone numbers?" they asked. "Why do you need to contact so many people?"

"I carry around those numbers," I said, "because I need them in my work. I work with all those people. So you can see I'm not alone. If anything happens to me, all these people will find out about it."

Then they came to that newspaper, that Nicaraguan paper. My heart stopped. It was such a stupid thing for me to be carrying, because I really had nothing to do with Nicaragua. I could have killed myself for being so stupid.

This old guy pushed his chair back and started reading the paper. "These bastards'll kill me now," I thought. But then I got up my courage. "No, I won't let these assholes make me piss in my pants. I won't let them get the best of me. I got myself into this mess, and I'll have to get myself out of it."

The old coot didn't say anything to me. He just laid back

reading the paper, while he sent me to the cell. Later at night he came to get me, and that's when the abuses started.

He asked me how I got that paper. I couldn't say who gave it to me, because that would create problems for them. So I said, "What paper? I don't know what you're talking about." I tried playing stupid.

"Don't give me that shit," he said. "Don't act like you don't know what paper I'm talking about. We found this paper in your purse." And he waved the paper in front of my face.

"Let's see it," I said, still pretending I didn't know what it was. But he wouldn't give it to me. "You know damn well what I mean. This rag that talks about the Sandinistas."

"Oh," I said, "I know what you must mean. One day I was in Tegucigalpa, and standing on the corner was one of those evangelicals—one of those religious people who always hand you things on the street. So I took the paper they were handing out and stuck it in my purse. But to tell you the truth, I never even looked at it. I thought it was about some religious group."

"Where did they give it to you?" he asked.

"In the Central Park," I said. "They were giving them out to everyone, so I took one, too. But I didn't even look at it."

"You think we're going to believe that?" he said. "What do you think we are, idiots? Now tell us about your connections with Nicaragua."

"Nicaragua?" I said. "I've never been to Nicaragua, and I don't even know any Nicaraguans. The only thing I know about Nicaragua is what I hear on the news, and it's not a crime to listen to the radio, is it?"

"Where does your organization get its funds?" he asked.

"Mostly from the campesinos. But we also get help from national and international groups," I said.

"Ah-ha," he said. "International groups. Which ones?"

"Don't you know," I told him, "that in Honduras there are groups called the United Nations, and the Food and Agriculture Organization? Those are the groups that help us."

He kept insisting that I was working with the Nicaraguans. He accused me of passing arms to Nicaragua, and of bringing arms in from Nicaragua to Honduras. And when I kept denying it, he got mad and sent for another man to come in and tie me up.

They tied my hands and feet together and hung me from the ceiling. They kept me hanging there for hours. When they untied me, they threw me on the ground and stomped on me.

Then they interrogated me again. They kept asking me what the campesino organization did, and how we were helping the Sandinistas. "That's how you get people to make up stories," I said. "They admit to things that aren't true so you'll stop torturing them. Well I'm not going to make up anything. You're accusing me of things I don't know anything about. We have nothing to do with Nicaragua; we're Hondurans fighting for our people's rights. Our problems are agrarian problems, and nothing else."

I was prepared for the worst but was determined to be strong. I said to myself, "What can these goons do to me? If they kill me, then let them kill me. At least I know I will have died for a just cause, I will have died for struggling on the side of the poor."

Since I was mentally prepared, I hardly felt the blows. They covered my mouth and hit me harder. Then they covered my mouth and nose so I couldn't breathe. And they threatened me with the *capucha*, that suffocating hood they put over your head.

"You better not do that," I screamed. "That's an abuse of my human rights. That's against the law and you'll be sorry." You see, we learned in our course on human rights that the capucha was against the law. And to my amazement, they didn't use it.

Then in the middle of the night, they tried to take me somewhere else. I knew that if they got me out of there, they would kill me and say that I disappeared. They would deny they'd ever been holding me. I knew I had to hang on a little longer, because I was sure my family and the CNTC were already looking for me. So I yelled and screamed and kicked and bit and wouldn't let them take me out of there.

Then one of the men tried to rape me. I got furious and said, "You'll have to kill me first." They didn't rape me, and they didn't move me either. But they kept me incommunicado for three days, with no food, no water, nothing.

They told everyone that came looking for me that I wasn't there. Meanwhile, the CNTC was fighting for my release. They made denunciations to the press and talked on the radio. So did other groups. Four days after I was arrested, my children heard on Radio América that I was in jail and came looking for me.

My daughter Lidia went to the DNI. She's a loudmouth like I am. When the DNI said they didn't know me, she shouted, "I know you're holding my mother and you better tell me where she is. I'm her daughter and I have the right to know where my mother is."

"We don't know who your mother is," they said, "and we don't know who you are, either."

"I don't care if you know who I am. I came to get my mother. I heard on the radio that you captured her and have her here."

"No, we don't know anyone named Elvia," they kept saying. "There's no one here by that name."

"The radio says you have her here," said Lidia, "and the radio doesn't lie. So why won't you admit that you're holding her? You think you're going to disappear my mother like you've done with so many others? Like you did with the union leaders, with priests and nuns? My mother has six children, and all of us will go shouting in the streets that you've disappeared our mother. If you don't tell me where she is right now, I'm going straight to the radio, to the press, and I'm gonna tell them what you're doing."

She went away, furious, and came back with our people from the union. And then they admitted that I was there. The next day the union returned with a lawyer and a court order, and the DNI released me.

I've been very sick ever since I was released. You see this gash in my leg? I've got another one just like it on my behind. It's from the officers' boots. It's from them stomping on me. The first week I was home my son had to carry me all around because I couldn't walk and I couldn't lie on my back either.

I've told my family and friends that I have some kind of disease. I swore to my son that it wasn't from being tortured. "Are you sure they didn't do anything to you, mommy?" he kept asking. "Yes," I told him. "They didn't touch me. It's just some disease I have." I didn't want him to get all upset and do something crazy. Besides, they warned me that if I told anyone what they did to me, they would come for my family.

One thing that's new is that ever since the Sandinistas came to power in Nicaragua, the military has started accusing us of being led by the Sandinistas, of working for the Sandinistas, of being Sandinista terrorists. I don't really know anything about Nicaragua. I've never been there. I've never met a Sandinista in my life. So where do they get this idea that we're Sandinistas?

Once they accused me of working with the Salvadoran guerrillas. They said someone in my union was passing arms across the Salvadoran border to the guerrillas. I said I didn't know what they were talking about. And I don't. They asked me what I thought of the war between the Salvadoran government and the Farabundo Martí guerrillas. I said I didn't know Farabundo Martí, and I didn't know what was going on in El Salvador. That's for the Salvadorans. We Hondurans have to worry about what's going on here in our own country.

They always try to say that we're part of some big conspiracy, when we're just a handful of poor campesinos. But let me tell you, when they keep asking you these things about other countries, it sure makes you curious about what's going on in those countries that they're so afraid of.

Another thing that's new is the anti-terrorist law. This Article 33, the anti-terrorist law, was approved by Congress last year. We protested the law, but it passed anyway. Before when we used to recover the land, we were charged with damaging private property. Now we're still charged with that, but also with being terrorists. The difference is that the terrorist charge is more serious; you can't even get out on bail with the terrorist charge.

Where do they get off calling us terrorists just because we try to recover the land? We don't want to hurt anyone. We don't even have weapons. So why do they call us terrorists?

If you want to know who the terrorists are, it's the landowners. They're the ones that hire thugs to kill us. They're the ones who get the DNI and the army after us. They're the ones who have us tortured, disappeared. Isn't that what terrorism is? Yet we're the ones who go to jail.

There are some people who try to protect us from the military. There's a human rights commission here, headed by a wonderful doctor named Ramón Custodio. You should see how that man defends people who've been captured. He gets on the radio and denounces the human rights abuses. He gives courses on human rights so that we know what our rights are.

This is very important to us. Because if we don't know what our rights are, we can't demand that they be respected. For example, I took a course that taught us that when we're captured by the DNI and held incommunicado, we can't be held more than 24 hours without being charged. And that if the DNI keeps someone incommunicado, we can get what they call a writ of habeus corpus, which says we have the right to know where that person is being held. They taught us how we could appeal to the court with this habeus corpus, asking them to present the prisoner. This is very important for us to know.

One time I was captured with Emilio, a poor campesino who didn't know anything. He wasn't even a leader; they just grabbed him because he was with me. The union got me out of jail, but he was still in there.

As soon as I got out, I tried to get him released. I said to the other union people, "Let's get one of those habeus corpuses for him." "Yeah," they said, "good idea." We went to one of the lawyers that helps us, and he wrote up a habeus corpus to present to the court.

The court sent its own lawyer to the DNI with the habeus corpus. I went with him. You can imagine how the DNI felt when I showed up with a lawyer from the court. They took us in to see the head officer. "Good afternoon," the officer said to us, all smiles. "What can we do for you?"

You sure get different treatment when you're with a lawyer, I said to myself. When we come in alone they either lock us up or throw us out on our ears.

The lawyer said, "I've come to look for a campesino named Emilio González. He was captured together with this woman." "No," said the officer. "I'm sorry but there's no one by that name detained here." "Oh yeah?" I said. "You captured me and Emilio on July 1, and you haven't released him yet. I know you've got him in jail here."

And the lawyer said to the officer, "I didn't come here to fight with you. I've come to fulfill this court order. I've come to find this man that you're holding here." And he read the habeus corpus act out loud.

The officer was mad. "Jesus Christ," he said, "I don't know why the judge writes these acts when he knows damn well how we operate around here. He knows how we work with the court. I don't know why he creates these scandals."

But the lawyer had guts. "I didn't come here to hear about how the DNI works with the court. I came to get this man you're holding. And if you refuse to present him, then I'll report it to the court. You've got the court order right there in front of you. Don't you know that it's illegal to hold someone more than 24 hours without any charges? Don't you know the law? Or do you think that when it comes to poor campesinos the laws don't apply?" I was proud of that lawyer. He had balls.

Then the officer changed his tune. He said they did have Emilio, but that he had just been captured yesterday, that he hadn't been held for 24 hours yet.

"What?" I said. "You've had him here six days now. And you took him for no reason, only because he was with me. Is it a crime in this country to be walking with someone else? Is that a crime? Because he didn't do anything."

The lawyer said, "Now you say you just captured him yesterday. And when we came in, you said he wasn't here."

"You see?" I said to the lawyer. "You see how they ignore the laws in this country and do whatever they please? That's how they disappear people. They capture them and kill them, and then they deny ever holding them. Well, we know Emilio is here. You can't do that to him."

Well, they finally handed him over to the lawyer. Thank God they didn't do anything to him; they didn't torture him like they did to me. Because the poor campesino really wasn't involved in anything.

So having that course in human rights has been very important to us. Otherwise we'd have never known about habeus corpus and all that.

I sometimes ask myself if we're really getting anywhere. Every time we win something, the army is on our backs— persecuting us, throwing us in jail, torturing us. So I don't know how much longer we can struggle through peaceful means. I don't know how much more we can take.

I've heard on the radio about these guerrilla groups that are fighting the government. One is called Lorenzo Zelaya Front, and the other is called Cinchoneros. Both the Cincho-neros and the Zelaya Front are clandestine and have been pretty inactive. (See Appendix 3 for more information on armed opposition.)

There was another group in about 1983 that was going to the hills to fight. I don't know what their name was, but there was a lot of news about them on the radio. The military found them and killed them all.

There was tremendous repression against the campesinos in those days. The military accused everyone of being part of this guerrilla group—which wasn't true. But they went ahead and rounded up campesino leaders, church workers like the delegates of the word, and union leaders. Some of the people they rounded up were killed. Others escaped to different countries or went into hiding. The rest of them were put in jail.

In 1986 the Congress was debating whether or not to let these prisoners go. The new president, Azcona, had just taken office, and we were all hoping he'd declare an amnesty. The prisoners went on a hunger strike to call attention to their problem, and all their relatives came to the capital to support them. Our organization, the CNTC, decided to support them, too. We knew they were just campesinos who'd been falsely accused.

So about 500 campesinos went to the Congress when the debate started. We listened to the politicians with their fancy speeches. Whenever they spoke in favor of amnesty, we applauded wildly. When someone spoke against it, we booed and hissed. Then they took a vote and the amnesty bill passed.

We were ecstatic! We sang the national anthem. Some of us sang with tears in our eyes; others were so choked up they couldn't even sing. It was beautiful.

Then we marched to the prison and people on the street joined us. We stopped the traffic and took over the streets, shouting *"El pueblo, unido, jamás será vencido!"*—the people, united, will never be defeated. By the time we got to the prison, we were 10,000 strong. It was a day I'll never forget.

I often wonder if the struggle in Honduras will end up being an armed struggle. In some ways it already is, except it's one-sided—because the landowners and the military that protect them are armed, but the campesinos aren't.

There are still a lot of people in Honduras who, like me, are determined to make changes through peaceful means. We know we have to first organize among ourselves, the workers and campesinos, and then try to make changes at the national level. I suppose that's why the government tries so hard to divide us. They know that once we have an organized people, an educated people, then we can start thinking about political parties and how to get a government in power that cares about the poor.

We're still determined to struggle through legal means—through protests, demonstrations, recoveries, dialogue. But if we don't get anywhere, we'll have to take the path the other countries in Central America have taken. We'll have to take up arms like they did in Nicaragua.

It's not something we're anxious to do, because we know how well armed the military is. And we see that every day there are more and more gringos in our country, more and more U.S. bases. We realize that if there is ever an armed struggle here, it will be the most barbaric massacre you can imagine. Because the Honduran military, thanks to the gringos, is armed to the teeth. And all the bases the gringos have built, all the weapons they've brought into this country, will be used against the Honduran people.

As for me, I'll continue my organizing work no matter what happens. I used to be afraid of the DNI. I heard all the horrible stories about what they do to you, and I was scared. But now that I've been there, I'm not scared any more. Now I know what to expect, and I know they can't break me.

Don't get me wrong. I don't want to go through that kind of thing again. I take precautions whenever I can. For example, there's one region where the landowners are after me. So when I go near there, I take a bus that doesn't make any stops. And I advise the campesinos beforehand that I'm coming so that two or three of them will be waiting for me when I get off the bus. When I'm in that area, I never go out alone.

But since I'm not willing to stop my organizing work, I'm sure someday I'll be captured again. If I'm lucky, they'll set me free. If I'm not lucky, they'll kill me. Every time I leave my house, I'm not sure whether I'll come back or not.

I'm ready for anything, and I'm not afraid to die. Because I know the campesinos will continue the struggle, and that my death will be part of that struggle. The only way they can stop me from what I'm doing is by killing me. But that won't stop the others from following my path. In that sense, I'm stronger than they are.

"You can't imagine how much hope it gives me to know that we have friends in the United States. Who would have ever believed it?"

Elvia with editor, Medea Benjamin.

14

Turn Your Tears into Strength

When I hear that all this military buildup in Honduras is just trying to maintain peace in our country, I ask myself what peace they're talking about. Maybe it's peaceful for the politicians. The congressmen make $3,000 a month; their bellies are full of food and drink; they've got a wad of bills in their pockets. So for them there's peace.

But not for the campesinos. Do you think a mother who can't send her children to school because she doesn't have any clothes to put on their backs feels at peace? Do you think a mother who watches her child die because she doesn't have a penny to take her to the doctor feels at peace?

To protect this great peace we have, the politicians have sold our country off to the United States. They've made us a colony of the United States.

They're only doing it, they say, to protect our national security. What national security? The national security they're protecting is that of their own big stomachs. They're protecting the fat checks that come pouring in from the United States.

If I had a chance to talk to Reagan, which of course I wouldn't since Reagan is only interested in talking to the rich, I'd tell him to take all the money he's sending to Honduras—all the guns, all the tanks, all the helicopters, all the bases, all the big, expensive projects he's financing—and get the hell out of our country.

We don't need the U.S. money. We never get to see any of it anyway. What do you think that money goes for? To the foreign bank accounts of the rich, to line the pockets of our corrupt politicians, to give the military more power to repress the poor.

It's the rich who need the U.S. aid, not the poor. We've lived for years with only our beans and tortillas, and we'll go on living with our beans and tortillas. If the U.S. stopped sending money, it would be the rich who'd be hurt, not us. They're the ones who live off the dollars.

All that money does for the campesinos is divide us. AID dangles some bills in front of the campesino groups to try to buy them off, to corrupt the leaders. It started this land titling program to say to some of the campesinos, "Stick with us and you'll get a piece of land. Don't worry about the others who have none." But the worst thing the U.S. money does is strengthen the Honduran military. For us campesinos this just means more repression, more human rights abuses, more disappeared.

We see the U.S. policy as very dangerous. The reason we haven't had a civil war here in Honduras is that we campesinos have had an alternative—our campesino movement. For us the political parties—the Liberals and the Nationalists—are all the same. As soon as they get into power they give all their friends jobs, and they start changing the laws as they please.

No, our only hope lies in the campesino movement itself. Any gains we've made have been thanks to our organizations, thanks to the fact that we work together. But if the United States is determined to break up the campesino movement, we'll be left with no alternative than to take up arms just like our neighbors have done.

And I hate to say it, but that's what I see happening. The United States is trying to draw us into a war with Nicaragua, but will end up drawing us into a civil war.

I must admit that sometimes I get so overwhelmed by the odds against us that I break down and cry. I see our children dying of hunger, and the ones that live have no jobs, no education, no future. I see the military getting more and more repressive. I see us being persecuted, jailed, tortured. I get exhausted by all the internal problems between the campesino organizations. And I see all of Central America going up in flames.

I start to wonder if it's worth it. I start to think maybe I should just stay home making tortillas.

But whenever I have these doubts, whenever I start to cry, I put my hands into fists and say to myself, "Make your tears turn into anger, make your tears turn into strength." As soon as I stop crying, I feel a sense of power go through my body. And I get back to work with even more enthusiasm, with more conviction than ever.

When I see some of my other compañeros get depressed, I say to them, "Snap out of it. Get back to work. We have too much to do to waste our time getting depressed." And they do the same to me.

One thing that gives us a great boost is when we hear that there are other people in other countries who are on our side.

Not long ago I was in a meeting with a group of Hondurans working for peace in Central America. Two gringos were visiting and joined the meeting. They weren't gringos from the United States. They were gringos from other countries I'd never heard of, some countries in Europe, they said. And they were here to show support for our struggle.

They asked me to write a message to the people in their country. I picked up the pen and I don't know how I did it—because I really don't write very well—but I wrote something and they understood it.

I wrote that I was just a poor Honduran, but that we were fighting for justice in our country. I told them how happy I was that there were people from other countries who were working for peace in Central America. I said I might not know what they look like, what language they speak, or even the names of the countries they come from, but that we were all brothers and sisters. I said that if we were both fighting for justice, then we were part of the same family.

These two gringo men were so touched by the message that they got up and hugged me and started to cry. Can you imagine gringo men crying? I never saw that in my life! So I started crying, too.

And I said to them, "Thank God there are people on our side. Thank God there are people on our side. Now we're really going to raise hell."

I later learned that there are also gringos in the United States who don't agree with their government's policies in Central America. It's amazing that Reagan has so much power and he still hasn't been able to conquer all the people in the United States. It shows he's not as powerful as we thought.

You can't imagine how much courage and hope it gives me to know that we have friends in the United States. Imagine that! Friends in the United States! Who would've ever believed it!

It's hard to think of change taking place in Central America without there first being changes in the United States. As we say in Honduras, *"Sin el perro, no hay rabia"*—without the dog, there wouldn't be rabies.

So you Americans who really want to help the poor have to change your own government first. You Americans who want to see an end to hunger and poverty have to take a stand. You have to fight just like we're fighting—even harder. You have to be ready to be jailed, to be abused, to be repressed. And you have to have the character, the courage, the morale, and the spirit to confront whatever comes your way.

If you say, "Oh, the United States is so big and powerful, there's nothing we can do to change it," then why bother talking about solidarity? If you think like that, you start to feel insignificant and your spirit dies. That's very dangerous. For as long as we keep our spirits high, we continue to struggle.

We campesinos are used to planting seeds and waiting to see if the seeds bear fruit. We're used to working on harsh soil. And when our crops don't grow, we're used to planting again and again until they take hold. Like us, you must learn to persist.

You also have to be fearless. If you begin with fear—fear of being persecuted or of going to jail or of being criticized—you might as well not start.

I don't know if it's the same in the United States, but here people are terrified that they'll be called communist. But if they call us communists, we have to tell them that that's a bunch of bull. We're not fighting for theories. We're not fighting for communism or Marxism. We're fighting for justice.

I'm always being criticized—that I'm a communist, that I'm a subversive, that I'm a whore, that I go around sleeping with all the campesinos, that I'm a bad mother, that I leave my children home alone, that I left my husband because I want to be free. Whatever. But we can't be afraid of criticism. We have to answer that we know where we're going and why we're going there, and if anyone wants to follow us, we'll be glad to show them the way.

You also have to be clear about your objectives, about why you're struggling. You can't struggle just because someone else tells you it's a good idea. No, you've got to feel the struggle. You've got to be completely convinced that what you're struggling for is just.

And then you have to have a plan. What are you trying to achieve? What methods will you use? How many people do you have? Who can you count on for help? How much money do you have? How long will it take you to reach a certain number of people? What will you ask them to do?

You have to begin educating people, telling them the truth about what's happening in the world. Because if the press in the United States is anything like it is in Honduras, the people aren't well informed. You have to teach them what's really happening in the United States, what your government is really doing. And once you've educated people, then get them organized.

Start out forming small groups, first in your own house, then with your neighbors. You might have to start out with just a handful of people—three women or three men. It doesn't matter if you start out small. Things that start out small get bigger and bigger. One group becomes two groups, two groups become four; and before you know it, you have a lot of well-organized people.

Then you start dividing up the tasks, and you make up your committees—the education committee, the women's committee, the youth committee. And soon you branch out to other neighborhoods and other villages and cities.

The other thing you have to do is make allies. I used to think you had to be poor to be part of this struggle. But there are people in Honduras who aren't poor, yet they're on our side. They're well-educated people—doctors, lawyers, teachers, engineers—who identify with the poor. I suppose it's the same in the United States. So don't only organize the poor and working people. You can also look for middle-class people, or even rich people who want to help change things.

But if you sit around thinking what to do and end up not doing anything, why bother even thinking about it? You're better off going out on the town and having a good time. No, we have to think and act. That's what we're doing here, and that's what you have to do.

I hate to offend you, but we won't get anywhere by just writing and reading books. I know that books are important, and I hope this book will be important for the people who read it. But we can't just read it and say, "Those poor campesinos. What a miserable life they have." Or others might say, "What a nice book. That woman Elvia sounds like a nice woman." I imagine there'll be others who say, "That Elvia is a foul-mouthed, uppity campesina." But the important thing is not what you think of me; the important thing is for you to do something.

We're not asking for food or clothing or money. We want you with us in the struggle. We want you to educate your people. We want you to organize your people. We want you to denounce what your government is doing in Central America.

From those of you who feel the pain of the poor, who feel the pain of the murdered, the disappeared, the tortured, we need more than sympathy. We need you to join the struggle. Don't be afraid, gringos. Keep your spirits high. And remember, we're right there with you!

Appendices

Appendices

HONDURAS FACT SHEET

POPULATION

— Total: 4,648,000 (1986) [1]—Urban: 39% (1985) [2]

—Ethnic make-up: 90% mixed
                7% Indian
                2% Black [3]

AREA

— 112,088 sq. km. (43,277 sq. mi.), slightly larger than Tennessee [4]

RELIGION

— 97% Roman Catholic; small Protestant minority [1]

HEALTH

— People per doctor: 3,120 (1980) [5]

— Percent of population with access to safe water: 44% (1980) [2]

— Infant mortality: 78 per 1,000 live births (1984) [1] (highest in Central America)

— Life expectancy: 61 years (1984) [6]

LITERACY

— 56% (1986) [1]

ECONOMY

— Currency: *Lempira*
Official exchange rate as of March 1987, two lempiras for one U.S. dollar.

— GDP per capita (1970 US$): $314 (1985) [7]

— Income distribution:
Top 10% of population receive 50% of national income
Bottom 20% receive 3% of national income [8]

— Labor force: 1.3 million; 62% agriculture, 20% services, 9% manufacturing, 3% construction, 5% other (1985) [1]

— Unemployment: 25-41% (1986) (25%: Honduran govt.; 41%: Honduran Economics Assn.) [9]

— Total Export Revenue: US$ 862.7 million (1985) [10]

— Major exports: 25.8% bananas, 23.9% coffee, 5.3% lead, 5.0% shrimp, 3.4% tobacco, 3.2% wood, 2.7% sugar, 2.6% meat (1985) [10]

— External debt:
US$2,392 million (1985) [7]
As percent of export earnings – 277% (1985)
— Percent of large firms owned by U.S. corporations:
100% of 5 largest firms
88% of 20 largest firms
82% of 50 largest firms [11]
— Agriculture:
Subsistence crops – 25% of arable land (1984) [2]
Cash crops – 52% of arable land (1984) [2]
Landless rural families – 125,000-150,000 (1985) [12]

SOURCES:

1. U.S. Central Intelligence Agency, *The World Factbook 1986* (Washington, DC: GPO, June 1986).
2. U.S. Agency for International Development, *Congressional Presentation FY 1987* (Washington, DC: GPO).
3. Latin America Bureau [Richard Lapper and James Painter], *Honduras: State for Sale* (London: LAB, 1985), p. 1.
4. *Hammond Citation World Atlas* (New York: Simon & Schuster, 1978).
5. World Bank, *World Development Report 1985* (New York: Oxford University Press, 1985).
6. World Bank, *World Development Report 1986* (New York: Oxford University Press, 1986).
7. *Central America Report*, August 22, 1986; data from Economic Commission on Latin America (ECLA).
8. U.S. Agency for International Development, *Congressional Presentation FY 1984: Latin America and the Caribbean* (Washington, DC: GPO).
9. Committee for the Defense of Human Rights (CEDOH), *Boletín*, No. 62, June 1986.
10. Banco Central de Honduras, Departamento de Estudios Económicos, *Boletín Estadístico*, July 1986.
11. Antonio Muiga Frassinetti, "Concentración Industrial en Honduras," in Tom Barry and Deb Preusch, *Central America Fact Book* (New York: Grove Press, 1986), p. 265.
12. J. Mark Ruhl, "The Honduran Agrarian Reform Under Suazo Córdova, 1982-85," in *Inter-American Economic Affairs*, Vol. 39, No. 2, Autumn 1985, p. 73.

HONDURAN CHRONOLOGY

1524 Spanish conquest of Honduras begins.

1821 Honduras wins independence from Spain as part of Central American Federation.

1839 Central American Federation breaks up, and Honduras becomes an independent republic.

1890 Banana companies are established. By 1913, bananas account for 66% of Honduran exports.

1905 U.S. troops land in Honduras for first time, in an unsuccessful attempt to protect conservative president Manuel Bonilla, who is overthrown by Miguel Dávila in 1907.

1911 With help of banana baron Sam Zemurray, Manuel Bonilla returns to presidency.

1932 Sixteen-year dictatorship of General Tiburcio Carias Andino.

1948 Former United Fruit Company lawyer Juan Manuel Galvez wins presidential election in which he is the only candidate.

1952 U.S. helps build professional army, including the opening of Francisco Morazán Military College.

1954 35,000 workers strike on banana plantations. Marks the beginning of broad, national-level union organizing, and the beginning of unions as a significant political force.
Conservative dictator Julio Lozano Díaz rules with iron fist.

1956 Army overthrows Lozano Díaz. Military junta takes power.

1957 Military gives way to elections. Liberal party candidate Ramón Villeda Morales becomes president and begins reforms in labor, welfare, and land tenure.

1961 Central American Common Market is established. Large increase in U.S. corporate investment in Central America.

1962 First agrarian reform introduced, and National Agrarian Institute (INA) created to oversee reforms. United Fruit Company forces Villeda to moderate reform plans.

1963 Villeda is overthrown in a military coup led by Colonel Oswaldo López Arellano, who takes the presidential oath with the president of Standard Fruit and the vice-president of United Fruit seated in the places of honor.

1965   López wins fixed elections to retain the presidency. With Nationalist backing, he rolls back Villeda's reform programs.
Peasant leader Lorenzo Zelaya and his followers are killed by the military.

1969   Tensions rise over peasant demands for land. Landowners and the government blame conflict on Salvadoran migrants in Honduras. Honduras attempts to expel 300,000 Salvadorans, leading to 100-hour "Soccer War" between Honduras and El Salvador. Results in end of Central American Common Market and marks entry of new, reform-minded leadership in the Honduran military.

1971   Conservative Ramón Ernesto Cruz, López Arellano's choice for president, is elected first civilian leader since 1963.

1972   Six campesinos occupying land at La Talanquera in Olancho are massacred.
Political infighting within civilian government and increased popular pressure for agrarian reform lead López to stage another coup, taking back power from Cruz. This time López decides to work with reformist movement, introducing collective bargaining, minimum wage, and broad land reform.

1974   Hurricane Fifi kills 8,000 and leaves 300,000 homeless.

1975   New land reform law passed.
United Brands pays $1.25 million bribe to Honduran economic minister in order to lower banana tax. As a result of "Bananagate scandal," López Arellano resigns and General Juan Mélgar Castro takes over presidency. Government increases repression. Fifteen peasant demonstrators, including two priests, are massacred at Los Horcones, Olancho.

1978   General Policarpo Paz García leads a military overthrow of Mélgar Castro and forms a military junta. Government characterized by rampant corruption.

1979   Sandinistas in Nicaragua overthrow Somoza regime. Marks beginning of closer ties between U.S. and Honduras.

1980   Lorenzo Zelaya guerrillas attack U.S. embassy in Tegucigalpa.
U.S. pressures Paz García to hold elections as a condition for receiving aid. Liberal Party wins Constituent Assembly elections.
Honduran soldiers and Salvadoran troops prevent hundreds of Salvadoran refugees from crossing Sumpul River; about 600 refugees killed.

1981   **March** Honduran Army prevents some 8,000 Salvadoran refugees from crossing the Lempa River into Honduras; some 200 refugees are drowned or killed.

Sept. Members of Lorenzo Zelaya guerrilla group shoot two U.S. military advisors and bomb the Honduran Congress.

Nov. Roberto Suazo Córdova of Liberal Party wins presidential elections. First time since 1971 that elected civilian government comes to power.

1982 Jan. Colonel Gustavo Alvarez Martínez, a close ally of CIA and contras, is named Chief of Armed Forces. Honduras begins to function as home base for contras. Internal repression on the rise.

Feb. The discovery of four clandestine cemeteries raises the issue of human rights abuses in Honduras.

April The government declares that strikes and land occupations are "subversive acts." Alvarez is promoted to general and human rights abuses increase.

June General Alvarez and President Suazo negotiate a major increase in U.S. military aid.

Sept. Cinchoneros guerrillas hold 83 hostages in Honduran Chamber of Commerce in San Pedro Sula; one political prisoner is freed, and guerrillas are flown to Panama.

1983 Feb. Big Pine I joint U.S.-Honduran military exercises begin.

Aug. Big Pine II military exercises begin.

Sept. 96 guerrillas with Revolutionary Party of Central American Workers (PRTC) ambushed by Honduran military. Most, including U.S. guerrilla Father James (Guadalupe) Carney, are killed.

1984 March Rolando Vindel González, leader of electrical workers' union, is kidnapped and disappeared. General Alvarez, head of Honduran Armed Forces, is overthrown by younger officers.

April General Walter López Reyes takes control of armed forces.

May 60,000 people demonstrate in Tegucigalpa and 40,000 in San Pedro Sula, protesting U.S. presence in Honduras.

1985 Jan. National Federation of Rural Workers (CNTC) is formed.

Feb. Big Pine III exercises begin.

Aug. Honduran army enters Colomoncagua refugee camp killing two Salvadorans, wounding fifty, and taking ten others prisoner.

1986 Jan. Honduran Armed Forces head Walter López resigns under pressure from right-wing officers. Col.

Humberto Regalado Hernández is named head of armed forces.

March Nicaraguan troops cross Honduran border in pursuit of contras. U.S. calls it invasion and sends Honduras $20 million in emergency aid.

May Cristóbal Pérez, leader of FUTH (United Federation of Honduran Workers), assassinated eight days after addressing massive May Day rally against contra and U.S. military presence in Honduras.

June U.S. Congress approves $100 million in aid to contras.

Aug. Home and car of radio journalist Rodrigo Wong Arevalo are bombed for Wong's criticism of military corruption and contra presence.
Home of alternate deputy Rodolfo Zelaya is raided by Honduran police in infighting over cut of contra aid money.

Sept. Office of Honduran Human Rights Committee (CODEH) bombed.

Dec. Honduras accuses Nicaragua of invading territory in pursuit of contras and retaliates by bombing Nicaraguan side of border.
Honduran Congress approves General Regalado for new 3-year term as head of armed forces.

1987 Jan. High-powered explosive destroys car of peace activist and labor leader Leonor Meza.

May Some 20,000 peasants demanding land participate in nationwide land recoveries and takeover of INA offices. Five peasants are killed in clashes with landowners.

SOURCES:

Central America Historical Institute, *Banana Cases to Contra Bases* (Washington, DC: CAHI, 1986).

Centro de Documentación de Honduras, *Boletín Informativo*, various issues.

Honduras Information Center, *Honduras Update*, various issues.

Latin America Bureau [Richard Lapper and James Painter], *Honduras: State for Sale* (London: LAB, 1985).

POLITICAL PARTIES AND ARMED OPPOSITION

POLITICAL PARTIES

Until 1979 the Liberal and National parties were the only legal parties in Honduras. However, there are few fundamental differences between the two. Traditionally, they have both been relatively conservative on social issues and in favor of foreign investment in their country, holding strong ties to the banana companies. In the last election campaign, some of the most crucial questions—such as the deteriorating standard of living, the contra presence on Honduran soil, the U.S.-sponsored military buildup, and tensions with El Salvador—were carefully not mentioned by any of the leading candidates.

The Liberal Party – *Partido Liberal (PL)*

The Honduran Liberal Party grew out of the anti-Spanish and anti-clerical reform movement of the nineteenth century, taking control of the country for the first time in 1876. Supporters of the Liberal Party have ranged from conservative landowners, through small farmers and the middle class in the countryside, to bankers and industrialists in the cities. The conservative wing, under the leadership of Modesto Rodas Alvarado, has been the more dominant force in the party since the 1960s. Rodas himself died in 1979; and in 1981 the Rodistas split into three factions: those who support Roberto Suazo Córdova, who ran the country from 1980 to 1986; those behind José Azcona Hoyo, who became president in 1986; and those loyal to Efraín Bu Girón, president of the Honduran Congress. The more progressive wing, known as ALIPO (People's Liberal Alliance), split up in 1984, leaving MOLIDER (Liberal Democratic Revolutionary Movement), a social democrat faction, separate from the original ALIPO group.

While traditionally viewed as the anti-military party, during the 1980s the Liberal Party has been closely aligned with the armed forces.

The National Party – *Partido Nacional (PN)*

The National Party was formed in 1919 in a split from the Liberal Party. The most conservative political party in Honduras, its support came originally from large landowners but now extends to other conservative

155

economic powers. Its ties with the military have traditionally been so close that it was often regarded as the "civilian wing of the armed forces."

Until the 1981 elections, the party was united behind Ricardo Zuñiga Augustinas. But after Zuñiga's defeat in 1981, the National Party also splintered. The faction called Movement for Unity and Change, like the Zuñiguistas, is in favor of keeping close ties to the military. There are other factions who favor more distance from the armed forces, such as the group led by Rafael Leonardo Callejas, who was the leading vote getter in the 1985 elections. (He did not win because the Liberal Party as a whole received more votes, thus by 1985 rules their leading candidate—Azcona—was the victor.)

Innovation and Unity Party – *Partido de Innovación y Unidad (PINU)*

Formed in 1969 after the war with El Salvador, PINU is a small moderate party supported by urban professionals and some labor leaders. It is the only party that has offered candidacies to peasant and labor leaders.

Christian Democratic Party – *Partido Demócrata Cristiano de Honduras (PDCH)*

The PDCH grew out of the peasant/student movement of the early 1960s. Formed officially in 1968, it is the most progressive of all Central American Christian Democratic parties. Its base of support comes from two major Honduran unions, the General Congress of Workers (CGT) and the National Campesino Union (UNC). The CGT is associated with the right wing of the party. The left wing was led by Efraín Díaz Arrivillaga, the sole Christian Democratic Congressional delegate. Efraín Díaz is a vocal critic of the country's Liberal and military rule.

Communist Party – *Partido Comunista de Honduras (PCH)*

The PCH is the most significant of several leftist parties in Honduras. Founded in 1954, it is also the oldest. It has a strong base in several trade unions. In 1981, it joined with the other leftist parties to form the Patriotic Front in an attempt to win assembly seats in the election.

Social Democratic Party – *Partido Social Demócrata (PSD)*

Formed in late 1986, this new party is a regrouping of social democratic politicians from other parties, such as MOLIDER and PINU. Its leaders include the brothers Jorge and Arturo Reina.

More Facts About Honduran Politics:

- Since its independence in 1821, Honduras has had 126 changes of government and 16 different constitutions.
- Even during the civilian rule of the 1980s, the elected president had less ultimate power than the head of the military. According to the Honduran Constitution, the army commander-in-chief has veto power over all cabinet appointments and all appointees' actions, and only he is able to give marching orders to the army.

ARMED OPPOSITION

The Cinchoneros Popular Liberation Movement – *Movimiento Popular de Liberación "Cinchoneros" (MPL)*

The MPL was formed by students from the National Autonomous University of Honduras right after the Nicaraguan revolution in 1979. They carried out political kidnappings and bank raids into the early 1980s, gaining recognition in 1982 when they hijacked an airplane and held a group of businessmen hostage in the San Pedro Sula Chamber of Commerce. In October 1986, they reportedly had a guerrilla band operating out of the northern department of Atlantida.

Revolutionary Party of Central American Workers – *Partido Revolucionario de los Trabajadores Centroamericanos – Sección de Honduras (PRTC-H)*

The PRTC-H has ties to the Socialist Party of Honduras (PASOH) and has counterparts in several other Central American countries. In July 1983, 96 guerrillas, led by Dr. Reyes Mata, attempted to set up a guerrilla base inside Honduras. Over 40 of them, including Father James (Guadalupe) Carney, a U.S. priest, were wiped out by Honduran counterinsurgency troops. By the mid-1980s, the PRTC-H was a very small, weak group, with most of its militant members either dead or in exile.

Morazanist Liberation Front – *Frente Morazanista de Liberación Nacional de Honduras (FML-H)*

The FML-H is the armed wing of the Communist Party-Marxist Leninist (PCH-ML), a group that split from the Communist Party in 1967. They take their name from Francisco Morazán, a Honduran national hero who tried to unite all of Central America in the 1800s.

Lorenzo Zelaya Popular Revolutionary Forces – *Fuerzas Populares Revolucionarias "Lorenzo Zelaya" (FPR)*

Like the Cinchoneros, the FPR was founded by students from the National University. The group gets its name from Lorenzo Zelaya, a Honduran campesino who was murdered by the military in 1965.

More Information About Honduran Armed Rebels:

- In 1983 the armed opposition created an alliance called the National Unitary Direction, but the alliance has not had a very profound impact.
- It is not clear how many of the actions attributed to various armed opposition groups are actually carried out by them. Many Hondurans speculate that a number of supposed guerrilla attacks were actually carried out by Honduran security forces as justifications for disappearances and other repressive measures.

SOURCES:

Barry, Tom, and Deb Preusch, *The Central America Fact Book* (New York: Grove Press, 1986), pp. 255-256.

Central America Historical Institute, *From Banana Cases to Contra Bases* (Washington, DC: CAHI, 1986).

Centro de Documentacion de Honduras, *Boletín Informativo*, various issues.

Honduras Information Center, *Honduras Update*, various issues.

Latin America Bureau [Richard Lapper and James Painter], *Honduras: State for Sale* (London: LAB, 1985), pp. 7-10.

LaFeber, Walter, *Inevitable Revolutions* (New York: W.W. Norton and Co., 1983), p. 298.

Peckenham, Nancy, and Annie Street, eds., *Honduras: Portrait of a Captive Nation* (New York: Praeger Publishers, 1985), p. 219.

MAJOR CAMPESINO ORGANIZATIONS

ANACH – Asociación Nacional de Campesinos Hondureños (National Association of Honduran Peasants)
ANACH was formed in 1962, with the help of the American Institute for Free Labor Development (AIFLD), to counter the strength of the leftist peasant group FENACH (Federation of Reform Cooperatives). After Villeda Morales came to power in 1963, FENACH was destroyed. ANACH quickly became the largest campesino union, with its greatest strength on the northern coast. Government figures estimate that ANACH has 23,000 members, and ANACH itself estimates it has 80,000 members. ANACH is the most pro-U.S. of the campesino unions.

CNTC – Central Nacional de Trabajadores del Campo (National Congress of Rural Workers)
The CNTC was founded in 1985 by independent and progressive campesino groups in an attempt to create a united movement for land reform. The following groups merged to form the CNTC:

- UNCAH (The National Authentic Campesino Union of Honduras)
- UNACOOPH (The Honduran National Union of Popular Cooperatives)
- FUCACH (The Honduran United Federation of Peasant Agricultural Cooperatives)
- FRENACAINH (The Honduran National Front of Independent Peasants)

CNTC is the most progressive of the four major peasant organizations. By January 1987 it claimed a total of 614 groups in 14 of the 18 departments of the country and a membership of 24,000. Unlike the other campesino organizations, the CNTC does not have government recognition and receives no government funding. While it is almost self-sufficient, it does receive some outside funding from groups like Oxfam Canada and England, the Swedish International Development Agency (SIDA), and the Dutch Humanistic Institute for Development Cooperation (HIVOS).

FECORAH – Federación de Cooperativos de la Reforma Agraria (Federation of Agrarian Reform Cooperatives)
FECORAH was created by the government in 1970 with groups that broke away from ANACH. It includes some 460

agricultural cooperatives with a total membership of about 16,000 people, according to government figures. FECORAH has its strength in the departments of Colon, Yoro and Choluteca. It is pro-government and conservative.

UNC – Union Nacional de Campesinos (National Campesino Union)

UNC is the second largest union, with 20,000 members according to the government and 75,000 members according to UNC. Its strength is in the departments of Choluteca, Olancho, Comayagua, Cortés, and Copán. It was formed in 1969 and was the first campesino group to organize land recoveries on a national scale. The UNC is co-founder of the CGT, the General Congress of Workers, which is an outgrowth of the Christian Democratic Party but is currently dominated by its conservative wing. Since receiving official government recognition in 1984, the UNC has been shifting towards the right. At its annual conference in 1986, the more progressive members were thrown out and decided to form their own organization, OCANH (Organización Campesina para el Agro Nacional de Honduras).

Peasant Women's Organizations:

Each campesino organization has its women's division. In addition, there is the women's organization **FEHMUC** (Federación Hondureña de Mujeres Campesinas – Honduran Federation of Campesina Women). FEHMUC was formed in 1977 in affiliation with the Christian Democratic Party. It carries out projects in health, agriculture, and handicrafts. In 1985 it split, with one faction forming **CODIMCA** (Committee for the Integral Development of Campesina Women). CODIMCA has bases in Copán and Ocotepeque.

SOURCES:

Benjamin, Medea, unpublished interviews with campesino organizations in Honduras.

Centro de Documentación de Honduras, *Boletín Informativo No. 64*, Agosto 1986.

Latin America Bureau [Richard Lapper and James Painter], *Honduras: State for Sale* (London: LAB, 1985).

U.S. ECONOMIC AND MILITARY AID
TO HONDURAS
(In millions US$)

YEAR	ECONOMIC	MILITARY	TOTAL
1979	29.1	2.3	31.4
1980	53.1	3.9	57.0
1981	38.5	8.9	47.4
1982	80.7	31.3	112.0
1983	106.0	48.3	154.3
1984	94.1	77.4	171.5
1985	215.2	67.4	282.6
1986	129.3	61.2	190.5
1987*	134.4	61.2	195.6
1988**	156.8	81.5	238.3

*Estimated.
**Proposed.

SOURCE: Agency for International Development (AID)
Congressional Presentations, various years.

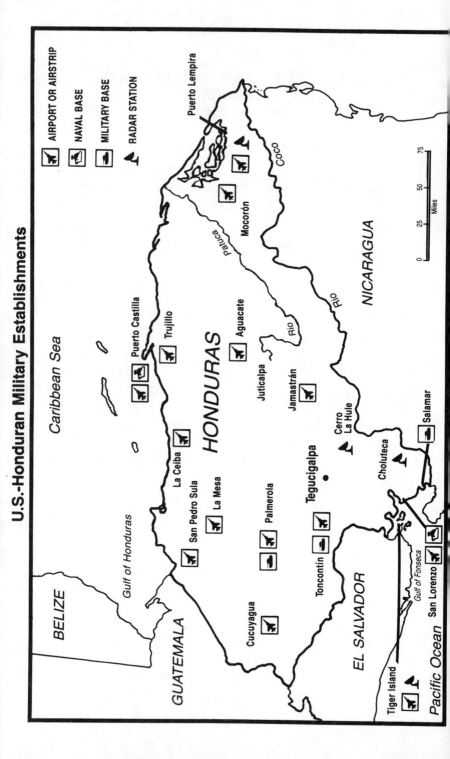

U.S.-Honduran Military Establishments

U.S.-HONDURAN MILITARY ESTABLISHMENTS IN HONDURAS [1]

Asterisks indicate sites of U.S. military construction between 1982 and 1986.

* **CUCUYAGUA:** Airstrip constructed to accommodate U.S. military C-130 transport planes.

   LA MESA: Airport of Honduran Air Force, used by U.S. military transport planes during Big Pine II maneuvers.

* **SAN PEDRO SULA:** Airstrip with capacity to handle C-130 transports.

* **LA CEIBA:** Air base and advanced ammunition depot. Recently upgraded runway.

* **PUERTO CASTILLA:** Permanent military port and air base. Former site of Regional Military Training Center, where Salvadoran and other Central American armed forces received training from Green Berets. Training Center was closed in 1985.

* **TRUJILLO:** Enlarged airport, used as a supply base for Puerto Castilla. Airstrip improved to handle C-130 military transport planes.

* **PUERTO LEMPIRA:** Secret satellite communication center. Airstrip upgraded to accommodate C-130 transports.

* **MOCORÓN:** Airfield improved to handle C-130 transports.

* **AGUACATE:** Airstrip extended during Big Pine maneuvers; has capacity to handle C-130 transports.

* **JUTICALPA:** Honduran National Training Center. Staffed initially by U.S. Special Forces. Will train 2,000–3,000 new Honduran recruits per year in the use of weapons and counterinsurgency tactics.

* **JAMASTRÁN:** Airport constructed during Big Pine maneuvers; has capacity to handle C-130 transports. Road and runway improvements during Big Pine 1987.

   SALAMAR: Base for advisors from U.S. Special Forces Mobile Unit.

* **CERRO LA HULE:** Radar station staffed by U.S. Tactical Air Command personnel.

CHOLUTECA: Radar station staffed by U.S. personnel observing and coordinating "contra" attacks across Nicaraguan border.

TONCONTÍN: International Airport for Tegucigalpa. Site of U.S. MILGP (Military Group) base. MILGP is responsible for all U.S. military training activities in Honduras.

* **SAN LORENZO:** Naval base and airport, now capable of handling C-130 transports. Facility for remotely piloted intelligence-gathering vehicles. Used to launch U.S. reconnaissance flights over El Salvador to detect guerrilla activity.

* **TIGER ISLAND:** Radar station staffed by 150 U.S. Marines. Monitors activity in Nicaragua and El Salvador. Has airstrip with capacity to handle C-7 transports. Also used as base for CIA speedboats.

* **PALMEROLA:** Site of General Headquarters for Joint Task Forces Bravo, with 800–1,200 permanently stationed U.S. troops. Base for Mohawk and Beechcraft surveillance aircraft used over El Salvador and Nicaragua. Primary forward munition and jet fuel storage depot for U.S. forces in region.

Additional Facts on U.S. Militarization of Honduras:

* In 1980, the U.S. had 25 military personnel in Honduras. By 1984, from 800 to 1,200 troops maintained a regular presence, with the bulk at Palmerola Base. [2]

* From 1983 to May 1987, almost 80,000 U.S. troops have been trained in Honduras on military maneuvers (approx. 20,000 in 1984; 22,000–23,000 in 1985; 23,000 in 1986; 13,400 in January–May 1987).[2]

* Between 1982 and 1986, the U.S. has built or upgraded in Honduras 11 airfields, 2 radar stations, roads, tank traps, fuel storage areas and air intelligence installations. [3]

SOURCES:

1. Camarda, Renato, *Forced to Move: Salvadoran Refugees in Honduras* (San Francisco: Solidarity Publications, 1985).

   Central American Historical Institute, *U.S. Military Construction in Honduras: 1982-1984* (Washington, DC: CAHI, 1984).

   Central American Information Center (San Diego), *Update*, Nov.–Dec. 1986.

Latin America Newsletters (London), *Mexico and Central America Report*, June 17, 1986.

LeMoyne, James, "U.S. Army Says G.I.'s Will Begin to Build 6th Airfield in Honduras," *New York Times*, March 3, 1986.

U.S. Senate, Appropriations Committee, Subcommittee on Military Construction, Minority Staff Report, *U.S. Military Construction Activities in Honduras*, April 4, 1986.

2. Food First, phone interview, Captain Ferrara, Marine Corps Desk, U.S. Pentagon.

3. LeMoyne, James, "U.S. Said to Plan a Long Presence in Honduran Bases," *New York Times*, July 13, 1986.

RESOURCE GUIDE

EDUCATION

American Friends Service Committee, 1501 Cherry Street, Philadelphia, PA, 19102, (215) 241-7159. Publishes pamphlets and research material on Central America. Their 30 regional offices throughout the United States seek to inform the public about developments in Central America.

Central America Research Institute, PO Box 4797, Berkeley, CA, 94704, (415) 843-5041. Publishes *Central America Bulletin,* a monthly analysis of issues related to Central America and United States involvement in the region.

Central America Resource Center, PO Box 2327, Austin, TX, 78768, (512) 476-9841. Serves as a clearinghouse for information on Central America and publishes *Central American Directory,* a listing of 1,100 organizations in the United States working to change United States policy in Central America.

Central American Historical Institute, Intercultural Center, Georgetown University, Washington, DC, 20057. Publishes *Update,* an analysis of news from Central America, and *From Banana Cases to Contra Bases: A Chronology of U.S.-Honduran Relations,* January 1977–July 1986.

Centro de Documentación de Honduras (CEDOH), Apartado Postal 1882, Tegucigalpa, Honduras. Publishes a variety of books on Honduras and *Boletín Informativo,* a monthly Spanish-language report on issues within Honduras.

Committee for Non-Intervention in Honduras, PO Box 641, Audubon Station, New York, NY, 10032. Publishes a bi-monthly bulletin and promotes Honduran speaking tours in the United States

Council on Hemispheric Affairs, 1900 L Street, NW, Suite 201, Washington, DC, 20036, (202) 775-0216. Publishes *Washington Report on the Hemisphere,* a bi-weekly publication on issues affecting Latin America.

Honduras Information Center, 1 Summer Street, Somerville, MA, 02143, (617) 625-7220. Publishes *Honduras Update,* a monthly collection of news and analyses of events in Honduras.

Institute for Food and Development Policy/Food First, 145 Ninth Street, San Francisco, CA, 94103, (415) 864-8555. Distributes books, action alerts, reports, and audio-visuals on internal developments in Central America and the effect of United States policy in the region.

Latin American Working Group, PO Box 2207, Station P, Toronto, Ontario, M5S 2T2, Canada. Publishes *Central America Update* and distributes books and educational materials on Latin America.

National Guard Clearinghouse, 438 N. Skinker, St. Louis, MO, 63130, (314) 727-4466. Coordinates information about National Guard and Reserve deployment in Central America and resistance to that deployment and other local military connections.

The Resource Center, PO Box 4506, Albuquerque, NM, 87196, (505) 266-5009. Publishes the *Resource Center Bulletin* and distributes books, booklets, and slide shows on Central America and the Caribbean.

Washington Office on Latin America, 110 Maryland Avenue, NE, Washington, DC, 20002, (202) 544-8045. A nongovernmental human rights organization monitoring events in Latin America. Publishes *Latin America Update,* a bi-monthly report with news from the region.

AID AND TRADE

MADRE, 853 Broadway, Room 301, New York, NY, 10003, (212) 533-0008. Gives material aid and promotes solidarity with mothers and children in Central America.

Oxfam America, 115 Broadway, Boston, MA, 02116, (617) 482-1211. A nonprofit international development and disaster relief organization that funds local grassroots groups in Asia, Africa, and Latin America. Currently supports nongovernmental Honduran organizations working to improve literacy, health, and food production.

Pueblo to People, 1616 Montrose, Houston, TX, 77006, (713) 523-1197. Works with Central American cooperatives selling handicrafts and promoting informational exchange between Central Americans and North Americans. Write for their free catalogue of Central American handicrafts.

World Neighbors, 5116 N. Portland, Oklahoma City, OK, 73112, (405) 946-3333. A private international organization working to create long-term integrated solutions to poverty through a strategy of stimulating local participation. Has been working with farmers in Honduras since 1981.

TRAVEL

The following organizations conduct travel seminars to Honduras and other developing countries that help North Americans gain a greater awareness of the causes and solutions to hunger in the Third World.

Center for Global Education, Augsburg College, 731 21st Avenue South, Minneapolis, MN, 55454, (612) 330-1159.

Food First Reality Tours, 145 Ninth Street, San Francisco, CA, 94103, (415) 864-8555.

Our Developing World, 13004 Paseo Presada, Saratoga, CA, 95070, (408) 379-4431.

BOOKS

Shepherd, Philip, and Mark Rosenberg, eds., *Honduras Confronts Its Future: Contending Perspectives on Critical Issues* (Boulder, CO: Lynne Reinner, 1986).

Shepherd, Philip, *The Honduran Crisis and U.S. Economic Assistance* (Boulder, CO: Westview, forthcoming 1988).

Latin America Bureau [Richard Lapper and James Painter], *Honduras: State for Sale,* (London: LAB, 1985).

Peckenham, Nancy, and Annie Street, eds., *Honduras: Portrait of a Captive Nation* (New York: Praeger Publishers, 1985).

For a list of books on Honduras in Spanish, write to Centro de Documentación de Honduras, Apartado Postal 1882, Tegucigalpa, Honduras.

Medea Benjamin

Medea Benjamin is the senior analyst on Central America and the Caribbean at the Institute for Food and Development Policy. Her reports and articles have examined U.S. foreign policy in the region, the roots of conflict in land inequities, and the struggle of the area's poorest to claim their own destiny.

Ms. Benjamin is co-author of *No Free Lunch: Food and Revolution in Cuba Today*, also published by the Institute. She has been a correspondent for Pacific News Service and her reports and articles have appeared in the *Los Angeles Times*, *Le Monde*, *Mother Jones*, the *National Catholic Reporter*, the *Village Voice*, *Third World*, *Food Monitor* and numerous other newspapers and magazines around the world.

Ms. Benjamin worked for ten years as an economist and nutritionist in Latin America, Africa, and Europe before joining the Institute. She has taken part in and evaluated projects for the United Nations Food and Agriculture Organization, the World Health Organization, the U.S. Agency for International Development, and the Swedish International Development Agency. She received a master's degree in nutrition from Columbia University and a master's degree in economics from the New School for Social Research in New York.

About the Institute for
Food and Development Policy

The Institute for Food and Development Policy is a not-for-profit research and educational center which investigates the root causes of hunger in a world of plenty. Also known by its imprint, Food First Books, the Institute studies the efforts of people around the world who are working to create food and farming systems that truly meet people's needs.

Founded in 1975 by Frances Moore Lappé, author of *Diet for a Small Planet*, and Joseph Collins, coauthor with Lappé of *Food First: Beyond the Myth of Scarcity*, the Institute has been hailed as "One of the most established 'food think tanks' in the country" by the *New York Times*.

The Institute has been credited with playing a key role in changing the global debate about the causes of and solutions to world hunger. Humanitarian responses to hunger, which formerly favored charity and development technology, now address issues of poverty and powerlessness—the underlying causes of hunger.

Member support and revenues from book sales account for 85 percent of the Institute's income. By accepting no contributions from government sources, the Institute is able to carry out independent research, free from ideological formulas and prevailing government policies. Known for their popularly written style and uncompromising analysis, Food First materials survey social conditions and development problems through a "food window," tackling subjects that range from population control to pesticides. In addition to books, these materials include a quarterly newsletter, reports, guides, audio-visuals, and informative leaflets known as Action Alerts.

Selected Resources From Food First

Books

___ *Don't Be Afraid Gringo: A Honduran Woman Speaks from the Heart* ($9.95)

___ *Help or Hindrance: U.S. Economic Aid in Central America* ($6)

___ *Nicaragua: What Difference Could a Revolution Make?* ($8.95)

___ *No Free Lunch: Food and Revolution in Cuba Today* ($9.95)

___ *Now We Can Speak: A Journey Through the New Nicaragua* ($4.95)

Audio Visuals

___ *Central America: We Can Make a Difference*
    ☐ Slide show ($52)   ☐ Filmstrip ($16)

___ *Faces of War* video cassette ($25)

Action Alerts

Visually dramatic leaflets with timely information on food and justice issues.
(Single copy $1; 5/$2; 25/$6; 50/$11.50; 100/$17; 500/$65)

___ *Central America: The Right to Eat*
___ *Nicaragua: Give Change a Chance*
___ *Honduras: The Real Loser in U.S. War Games*

━━━━━━━━━━━━━━━━━━━━━━━━━━━━━━━━

☐ Please send a free Food First catalog.

☐ I want to become a member of Food First. Enclosed is my tax-deductible contribution of $25 or more.

Minimum order $2.

$_____ amount of order

$_____ 6% sales tax for Calif. residents

$_____ 15% postage and handling

$_____ Total enclosed

NAME _____

ADDRESS _____

CITY _____ STATE _____ ZIP _____

FOOD FIRST BOOKS • 145 Ninth Street • San Francisco, CA 94103 • (415) 864-8555

Pledge of Support

To the President of Honduras:
Having read the book *Don't Be Afraid, Gringo,* the story of Elvia Alvarado, I am deeply concerned about the fate of Elvia and others like her who are working for justice in your country. I urge you to protect their rights of free speech and free assembly, and to ensure that their human rights are not violated.

_____
SIGNATURE
_____
NAME
_____
STREET
_____
CITY, STATE, AND ZIP
_____
PHONE

Mail to: Elvia Alvarado, c/o Institute for Food and Development Policy, 145 Ninth Street, San Francisco, CA 94103. We will hold these letters and send them to the president of Honduras if necessary. Thank you for your support.